ADVANCED LAKE FLY FISHING
THE SKILLFUL TUBER

Robert Alley

Frank Amato Publications
Portland, Oregon

Dedication:
To my dad, family, and my many friends in Sacramento.
Thanks for your support!

Cover Photograph by Brad Jackson
Flies Courtesy of Frank Flowers
Book Design and Art: Tony Amato
Typesetting: Charlie Clifford

ISBN: 0-936608-97-8 (Softbound)
ISBN: 0-936608-98-6 (Hardbound)

Printed in U.S.A.

Contents

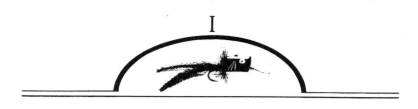

The Three Main Problems Confronting Float Tubers

I think of float tubing as "vertical swimming." The kicking motions of my legs are almost the same when I swim in "freestyle" but, with a tube seat suspending me in a sitting position, I can look around and use my arms for casting. Since swimming is as natural for me as breathing, I've never been afraid of water therefore I quickly grew to love the subtle sport of float tubing.

In my "round boat," I not only gain a whole new view of a lake but I also have greater control of my actions than when I fly cast from the shore or in a boat. Instantly, I am able to swivel myself to any point of a circle, face it, and cast in that direction. I always have my ears "tuned" for little noises like a trout smacking the surface, a tail of a fish swishing in the shallows, minnows diving in and out of the water, land creatures plopping into the lake, and birds dipping in the surface film. Quickly, I turn toward these signs of feeding trout or bass and I am ready to cast toward it. I also avoid putting flies in high tree branches. When I snag down deep, I move directly on top of it and, most of the time, pull the fly off the bottom. It helps not to react too vigorously when the fly hooks on underwater cover. The best thing about tubing is being able to cast and kick at the same time, which, if I avoid excessive false casting, allows the fly to stay in the water for long periods of time therefore increasing my odds to catch more fish. In a canoe, the man in the rear is constantly altering the direction of the boat even in a slight wind. Most canoeists don't like anchors and for good reasons. The extra weight is troublesome and in small ones space is a problem. Therefore, in canoes, somebody has to divide his or her time between fishing and paddling. Yet, I love the invigorating quiet strokes that are associated with canoeing. When I visit my family in Virginia, I like to fish with my brother-in-law, Ken Townsend, and paddle around in his 17-foot canoe. I also like motorboats. When I was a teenager and lived in Virginia, I enjoyed cruising in our 12-foot cartop boat, but I disliked the anchoring process and rowing when the gas or electric motor failed to start. I have read of tubers who use a small boat to quickly get around a big reservoir and then leave it to float tube. I think that's a great idea! But, until I can afford one, I enjoy the advantages of quickly moving around in a circle to work an area thoroughly, storing my "boat" in my walk-in closet, (inflated — always ready to go), launching virtually anywhere, and fly casting as I kick around a lake or pond.

My first day in a float tube didn't automatically, let me catch two-foot trout. There isn't one piece of gear from a sinking line to the hottest pattern or new-fangled boat that guarantees big fish. Modern equipment is helpful, yes, but the most important thing is learning how to use it well and also learning the proper fishing techniques. Equally as important is constant observation and experimentation. It is human to fall into routines and ruts. It happens to me more than I like to admit. Nearly always I start with a Wet Cel II sinking line, a 4X tippet, a small dull or dark Woolly Worm or nymph, and an ultra-slow retrieve because at least 75 percent of the time it works best. But, as hours tick away, and such methods aren't working, I must stop, analyze what is wrong, observe, and make corrections. In terms of fishing method and effective imitations of natural insects, I now change more readily than when I first began fly fishing. I now know that for most insects like damselflies, mayflies, caddisflies, and midges (the four most common groups of lake insects) there are a number of patterns to imitate one species or order. For example, the Hares Ear nymph, brown Woolly Worm, Whitlock wiggling damsel nymph, and Janessan Damsel nymph all do a good job imitating the naiad of the damsel fly. Most of the time I do well with the first two, but when educated browns and rainbows pass up those two artificials, I need the more exact pattern which Hal and David tie. When the usual slow retrieve fails to work, I immediately change to other ways to bring the fly back toward me. Even though I now own two Battenkill IV reels and four extra spools, I seldom deviate from the Wet Cel II line even when it's obvious I need a faster sinking line to reach the bottom or when the Wet Cel II digs too deep in the underwater weed beds. Silly, huh? I own all this fancy gear and half of it merely takes up space in a gear bag. Although I need more experimenting, I'm now realizing a Wet Cel I does better in the four-foot depths than the Wet Cel II.

Since my first trip in my tube, almost 10 years ago, I found there were three problems that confronted me and I accepted the challenge of dealing with them. The first is timing myself back to the car when day becomes night or hovering close to the shoreline when thunder and lightning boom and streak across the sky. Throughout the day it is a good idea to keep track of the time and to observe the ascent and descent of the sun and how long it takes to reach different sections of a lake. Use points of coves, beaver dams, manmade structures, brush piles, beds of rocks, and coves as guideposts and note how long it takes to get from one to the other. Once this process is habitual, when it's late afternoon, it's fairly easy knowing when to turn around, and (if possible) fish the opposite shoreline back to the car. I tube as far from the car as possible since I often find areas where shoreline anglers are unable to fish. After 8:00 p.m. on a summer evening, if I am within 15 minutes of my car, I cast my flies into good cover and enjoy the best time of day worry-free until the skies are dark. But, if at 8:00 p.m., I am at least 30 minutes from where I parked, I need to kick at top speed until I at least see the wagon or am close to it. Then I fish until dark.

When I fish lakes under 100 acres, I seldom worry about timing since the car is seldom far away. In a later chapter, I intend to show how to work big reservoirs.

Storms usually manifest themselves early as they approach the lake. I'm more of a daredevil than I realized. It often takes a summer thunderstorm to wake up the trout and make them feed especially when the surface water layer is over 70. It is difficult to leave when suddenly rainbows or browns to 18 inches hit my fly and streak to the depths of a lake.

Early and late in the season, I use a heavy nylon-shell garment. I prefer it over the wader because neoprene waders roll up easier next to the body and polypro top and bottom than over a thick coat. With it outside the wader, it protects me better from rain or waves because the water rolls back to the lake rather than alongside my back! Although wool is warm it also absorbs water. Therefore it doesn't help when rain pounces down unless it is used for warmth underneath the wader and a rain slicker is on the outside but with neoprene the combination, for me, is bulky.

In warm months, a nylon windbreaker works well, but avoid those with a cloth inner lining – it holds in sweat. When sitting in a tube, even the edges of short garments become wet so I have a second jacket in the car for warmth on cold evenings after I'm off the lake. The price of Goretex coats has prevented me from trying them. They are considered the ultimate for warmth and keeping anglers dry, but I've been reasonably happy with my system.

Wind is the second problem confronting anyone who tubes or fly fishes. Yesterday, before starting this book, I went to Rancho Seco Lake where strong winds provided fun and excitement for the sailboaters but brought me only frustration! In my Buck's Bag float tube, with a solid windbreak around me, the wake seldom hit me, but kicking against it was difficult. Despite three-foot waves, I persisted by angling into the wake rather than heading directly into it. If I quit every time a strong wind frothed a lake, I'd miss many good fishing opportunities.

Nearly all the articles or books I've read about fighting wind advise the use of eight or nine-weight rods but I have found that learning to cast high and fast — the HS/HL method — does more than purchasing the heavy rods. I believe, after using six-foot wands for five-weight lines to seven-weight rods of eight-and-a-half feet, that rod length is secondary to casting correctly. It is possible that combining long rods with the HS/HL casting style is the best idea, but, on the whole, I've been pleased with my Orvis All-Rounder which takes a seven-weight line and is eight feet, three inches long. By snapping the backcast to just past the 12:00 position, pausing only momentarily to allow the line to straighten, and then driving it forward toward the 9:00 position, I am able to reach to 40 feet in wind and 70 feet in calm conditions. As Pat Sullivan of Tempe, Arizona coached me, "Drive the line forward as if you were hammering a nail." Adding a strong haul on either the forward or backcast increases the speed of the line and eliminates much false casting. In the strongest wind, I keep my casts short (under 30 feet). Most of the time, though, when using a sinking line, I want long casts which then become long retrieves because I can cover a lot of water and underwater cover, but when I use a floating line, I usually find shorter casts are better.

When the wind becomes strong, there are several ways to fish. Yesterday, at Rancho Seco Lake, when I faced the shoreline, I sliced the line across the wind and slightly upwind. Using Woolly Worms or nymphs, I think of this method on par

Fishing In The Wind

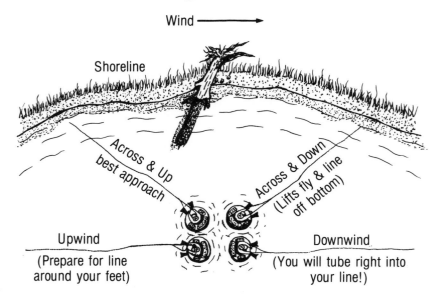

Wind ⟶

Shoreline

Across & Up
best approach

Across & Down
(Lifts fly & line
off bottom)

Upwind
(Prepare for line
around your feet)

Downwind
(You will tube right into
your line!)

with casting upstream and dead drifting the flies. The main difference is that, with the sinking line, I let the belly straighten out and then inch the fly back toward me. Sometimes trout follow and hit the fly close to the tube. For that reason I bring the fly back to within a few feet of the tube. The easiest thing to do is cast downwind but, if I don't think fast and swivel out of the way, my legs and feet can tangle in the line as I drift toward it. It also means a fast retrieve which usually is unproductive and keeps the fly off the bottom where good-sized trout and bass usually stay. Casting directly upstream presents the same problems. The most effective technique is to angle the cast into the wind since a fly can be crawled on the bottom. In fact, with this method, the belly of the sinking line helps to induce a good presentation of the fly. But to cast across the waves and in the direction in which they are going creates a belly that lifts the fly from the bottom keeping it away from the "fish zone." It isn't easy to stay on a lake when the wind is raging, but frequently such weather creates good fishing. I recall many days in the mountain lakes of Arizona when the water temperature was over 70 and fishing was dreadfuly slow until the wind whipped across the lake and rejuvenated the trout which had been hiding under rocks and weed beds. During such windstorms I often took two and three-pound trout on every tenth cast. The best fishermen are those willing to tough-out bad weather conditions.

The third problem to overcome is cold water. While trying to be comfortable in all water temperatures, I have worn three different kinds of waders, several different types of pants and shirts, and four types of fins. My system still isn't perfect, but now, I do reasonably well in water down to 45 degrees. I started with Red Ball waders which were comfortable, light, and great for wading streams, but despite Long Johns, when lakes dropped below 60, my lower body chilled. In a year they wore out, because they were too thin and couldn't take the pressue of being sat upon all day. With extra-thick Seal Dries, I was comfortable until water dipped below 55. After two years the seams split. Should I blame the material or my expanding waistline? Since then, I have been wearing James Scott neoprene waders. Without polypropolene underwear I am comfortable down to 50, but with it on I am warm in water down to 45. Whether I fish a valley lake for bass or a mountain lake in early spring, I always wear the bottoms because I don't like the feel of neoprene wrinkling against my skin and jeans tend to buckle up underneath them. When air temperatures stay below 65, I add the polypro top, a long-sleeve cotton shirt with a collar, and a jacket. The biggest trouble with neoprene (beside the cost) is staying in reasonable shape. Although it stretches, too much girth strains the material and flexibility is lost.

Fins have been my biggest frustration. Originally I purchased cheap K-mart fitted fins which worked and I liked them since the whole foot was protected, but when I bought rubber booties to add warmth to my feet, even the largest fitted fin was too small. I then tried fins that laced like a street shoe, but the following year the rubber around the grommets tore and I needed a new pair. I then chose the power fin which was heavy and clumsy to enter through the leg holes, but once I was on the water, they moved me along with minimal kicking effort. With strong strokes, the power fin cut through high wake quickly. But one day, after a year of using them, I scuttled along the bottom of Becker Lake in Arizona and my right foot suddenly lightened. Despite having cinched up the strap, the fin loosened as I pushed myself off the bottom and it fell off my foot. I spent the rest of the afternoon searching for it, but I never found it. I often wondered if anyone hooked and retrieved it.

I then bought the Force Fin which I still use. It is almost perfect! It is short, lightweight, goes easily through the leg holes, provides good power, and walks as easy as a street shoe. But it sinks if it slips off the foot. (Bob Evans, the manufacturer of the fin, tells me he is in the process of making a floating model.) I think a fin tether is a better idea and it should be in all sizes up to calves of 20 inches or more. One cheap one I bought fell apart. I tried old fly line but the knots are difficult to undo at the end of the day. James Scott makes one out of velcro but only in one size (now in 1990, I don't know if they still make it). Both the zippered and velcro bootie are too narrow for my feet and neoprene wader so I slip a sock liner over the heel and then put on the fin. In cold water, (below 55) I wear my polypro sock. This present system works well about 85 percent of the time, but I now work on the other 15 percent!

With each new season, I tackle these three problems — timing, wind, and cold water—and look for new solutions. Some writers discuss problems such as relieving oneself or launching a tube, but I don't understand what bothers them. Because I fish the edge where the lake's bottom dips toward deep water, I am usually close to the shore where I can walk out, lower the waders and do what comes naturally. I walk in and out of lakes and ponds while in the tube which is strapped over my shoulders. Sometimes mud or slick rocks slow me and I must watch carefully where and how I step, but this is only a matter of being patient and thoughtful. Once I am sitting in my tube, I slip the strap off my shoulders but leave it attached to the "D' rings and either let it dangle behind or stow it under the stripping apron.

I think most solutions to float tubing problems whether they be timing, wind, or cold water relate to using common sense and being logical and orderly. Having the proper gear and attire definitely helps but how it is used is much more important.

Choose Your
Trout Lake Wisely

I know that when "fishing fever" strikes most of its victims impulsively dash for the first lake that they think of, but, with a few minutes of careful thought, the angler can increase his or her odds for a fish-filled day.

It doesn't matter on which coast the fisherman lives. The 10 factors that influence his choice are still the same: altitude, water temperature, water height, water clarity, lake size, maximum depth, configuration, type of lake, available cover, and insect activity.

On the East Coast, it is rare to find stillwaters above 6,000 feet in elevation which is relatively low to many westerners. In late May, lakes can reach into the 70s when the East experiences a warm spring. Such a condition may seldom be witnessed by a Rocky Mountain fly rodder or not seen in the Sierra Nevada Mountains until July. I know there are many areas where the kind of lake, altitude, and amount of cover are limited, however, one should consider the factors that are the most applicable and make a conclusion based on the known facts.

Nearly all these factors determining this important decision relate to each other. The altitude affects the temperature which also determines the amount of weed growth and potential for insect activity. But it becomes trickier: Large, deep impoundments take longer to warm than small ones. A reservoir that sprawls to infinity with an endless number of arms and coves of varying depths is likely to have various surface temperatures in different locations at the same time. If a body of water is exceptionally low or high, the average depth of a lake changes to affect not only where the fish roam but also how quickly or slowly it warms or cools. Smaller bodies of water are the most influenced by great variations of water level. Generally, I find, when water of 50 degrees or more crests well above normal levels, the trout work their way toward the banks but spread out and are difficult to find. When lakes dwindle in size and become low, the trout seek deeper water and tend to congregate. My preference is to have the reservoir just a bit on the low side and clear so that when I do find the trout I can frequently stay in one place for hours catching browns and rainbows. Exceptionally high and dirty water creates lousy fly fishing and if it's possible, I avoid it. However, once, on a lake in Arizona, I persisted despite it looking like pea soup and I caught a 19-inch brown weighing almost five pounds.

Most writers agree there are two types of lakes — seepage and drainage. A seepage lake is a standing body of water which originates from springs or rain water whereas a drainage lake has an inlet and outlet, technically a reservoir which dammed a river or stream. The potential for the latter is greater because such stillwaters are more stable and fluctuate less throughout the year creating fairly permanent environments for trout. Small drainage waters are more susceptible to wide variations of water level because they often lack deep water. Here in northern California, 95 percent of the trout impoundments are of the drainage type and there are literally hundreds from sea level to elevations over 10,000 feet. As a float tuber, a larger lake is over 500 acres. Deep water, for me, is over 30 feet.

Air And Water Temperature Chart
(Based on Arizona and California Mountain Lakes)

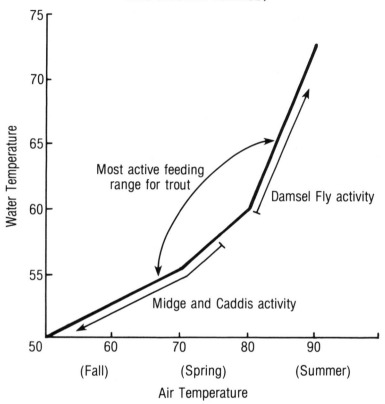

SPRING

I define it when the air temperatures stabilize above 70 degrees when water at a given altitude is 50 to 55 degrees. This usually translates into active trout and good fishing. The trick is to find that altitude level which approximates this weather condition. However, the size and depth also come into consideration because large reservoirs tend to warm slower than small ones, therefore the smaller places are better early in the year. Here in California, there are many such Sierra Nevada mountain lakes so I need to narrow the scope further. Seepage lakes are better early in the year. Most insects prefer weeds and other sorts of cover. This fact tells me to pick a lake with a good range of "structure." Circular reservoirs not only are tedious to fish but can't compete with lakes that have many arms and coves. The latter invariably have a good mix of shallows and depths allowing the trout to move between the resting spots on the bottom and move up into the upper food-producing levels.

Here in Sacramento, within two hours of my apartment, I can reach lakes from almost sea level to 7,000 feet. It is now March and the weather has been extraordinarly warm. Here in the valley, temperatures have stabilized over 70 degrees yet in the mountains it is 10 to 15 degrees cooler so I just decided to stay in the valley although the foothill lakes are almost warm enough to provide good action. These are reservoirs from 1,000 to almost 5,000 feet in altitude. Over that, I'm in the mountains.

I think the most about a lake's size, depth, water level, configuration, and cover. The best trout impoundment closest to me is not only huge but also relatively limited for cover and insect hatches therefore I just cross it off my mind. A place with good range of cover and depths comes to my mind, but it is mainly a bass lake and my thought processes are stuck on trout. Almost all the valley waters are stocked with rainbows, but only a scattering of those lakes are deep enough to carry the fish over through the hot summer. To catch the larger ones during our "cold" season and in the spring, I have to make a compromise. I know of a reservoir about 70 miles toward the coast which is big, quite deep, and has many arms and coves but is relatively limited to the amount of cover available. It is also low in elevation therefore it should be at a good temperature for trout. If I'm smart, for now in March, I ought to go to Lake Berryessa. But I'm not always smart. Sometimes a certain lake calls me and I go there regardless of the factors.

SUMMER

It is my favorite time of year. I define it when the air stays above 80 degrees and the trout waters have reached 60 degrees or just over. When I make a good choice, I have excellent fishing. If air temperatures remain above 90 degrees for too long, the surface layer (thermocline) of most stillwaters can climb into the low 70s and the trout become dormant and almost impossible to catch. During these sunny days, I haunt my favorite trout "holes" above 5,000 feet. When the hottest weather arrives in late July and August, instead of going to high altitudes of 9,000 feet I usually stay in the mid-range reservoirs. They not only have strong currents for the river flowing through it but also are protected by the shade of the pine trees crowding the shoreline.

In May, when the "large ponds" are sprouting with weeds and trout eat Callibaetis mayflies or damselflies, my choice is a small fish-for-fun lake. In June, Prosser Lake competes with it. Loon Lake and another small fish-for-fun lakes are usually good in July and August. In September the weather can be almost anything. Most likely, I can be found on one of my favorite places where, because I know it well, I can enjoy a good fishing day.

FALL

As far as I'm concerned, this is the best time of the year to fish the Sierra Nevada Mountain lakes. The weather has now settled to near 60 degrees and the water hovers near 50 degrees as the trout enjoy their last supper before hibernation. From October to the end of the year, I work down in elevation with the intent of always fishing places where the trout are active. But it doesn't always happen that way!

November almost always ends the mountain fishing and begins the foothill season. I have yet to do well in these lakes most of which have steep banks, minimal weed beds and insect hatches. They contain other fish species and I have taken smallmouth bass, bluegill, and even a few sucker on flies.

IN CONCLUSION

December through March I stay in the valley and try to decide which lakes offer me the most types of cover, ranges of depths, and coves. Most of the time, I pick the smaller reservoirs since they tend to stay a bit warmer than the big ones.

Walking into my favorite fly shop is fun, but like my fellow fly fishers, I can be as cynical and suspicious as anyone else. Especially when the report for Folsom Lake, 25 miles from my apartment, is that "arm-long rainbows are attacking flies on every cast." Most anglers, I think, rely too much on the weekly reports by newspaper fishing columnists who may have obtained their reports from heresay rather than actual fish counts. Use the 10 factors and the head on your shoulder and your days may become more fishful!

In Search Of
Active-Feeding Trout

It is now early May and the weather in the Sacramento Valley has stabilized above 75 degrees. My eyes leave the typewriter keys and, as I gaze out the window, I know I need to write less and fish more. Despite the frustrations, as each day passes writing novels, short stories, and fishing books becomes not only more satisfying but also more meaningful to me. Thinking of my 10 factors, I try to decide which lakes would have active trout. In the foothills the sun is nearly as strong as it is in the valley, but near Truckee, almost 6,000 feet up, the air only warms to about 60 degrees. I think of my favorite mountain lake, and its browns and rainbows to almost eight pounds obsess me. Those Sierra Nevada mountain trout are probably just awakening from the lethargic spell of winter. A foothill reservoir is more likely to be the best bet, but I'm only familiar with a few and they aren't the kind of lake I like. Steep cliffsides jut into them and provide few weedbeds for insects and crustaceans. Now, after pursuing lake rainbows and browns for almost 10 years, I conclude that how ever troublesome weeds can be such greenery is absolutely necessary for the food trout love to eat. I have yet to catch a trout over a foot in stillwaters that didn't provide good populations of insects, bugs, and other such tidbits. Obsessed with trout, I refused to think of the smallmouth bass that also swim in many of the mid-elevation reservoirs. When I fish the valley lakes, I think of bass because, for the longest part of the year they provide the bulk of the sport for anglers. From November to April, stocked rainbows are active and keep dedicated fishermen from catching the "winter blues" as they wait for the high lakes with wild trout to thaw out. Frequently, the rainbows hide in deep water in the summer where they grow and put on pounds. Both Folsom and Lake Berryessa provide trout to six pounds during the winter. The trick is to find the schools of rainbows in these two huge watery worlds. Now in May, the trout fishing in the valley is coming toward an end. I have yet to delve into this fishy subject. Even in Sacramento, winter is not my favorite time of year for outdoor activity, but I'm glad snow and ice don't exist here. My thoughts return to my favorite fish-for-fun mountain reservoir with the big browns and rainbows. I may be asking for a slow day but I just decided to fish it.

After a two-hour drive, I opened the door and cold air attacked my skin. Looking over the hood of my car and across the little body of water, I noted three other tubers and several boaters at the upper end. Twenty minutes later, I was rigged up and I 'kicked away from the shoreline as I went through my usual routine which prepared me for the day. After attaching the clip of the net retriever to a "D" ring on my right side, I hooked the stripping apron together and slipped my net underneath it. With my two rods in my right hand, I reached for my thermometer and thermometer stringer from the top left pocket of my tube and slipped the thermometer onto an end loop. I lowered it into the water after attaching the stringer to a "D" ring on my left side. With pliers I eliminated the middle loops. After I cinched the five-weight rod rigged with a floating line under tube straps, I worked out some line and, with my Orvis All-Rounder, I made my first cast of the day. My first six or eight casts unkink my arm and shoulder muscles as I look around trying to decide where to fish. Then I cast into deep water, held the rod underneath my right armpit, and checked the water temperature.

"Forty-eight! How can that be?"

I returned the thermometer to the water but my second reading was the same as the first. For a moment, I wished I were on a foothill lake where the water would be at an ideal reading for trout activity but then I realized the potential for good fish was better here.

I have caught trout, even browns, when a lake hovered near 44 degrees, but for most places I have fished, the most active feeding didn't begin until the surface layer stabilized above 50 degrees. Shaking in the cool air of mid-morning, I reflected that the thin air at this elevation cooled considerably more than the slightly thicker valley air and that might account for the lake being colder than I expected. I turned around and finned toward the shoreline and discovered the two-foot shallows reached to 50 degrees. Facing the shoreline, I fished a Zug Bug close to the bank but, an hour later, after another fly change, I worked the deeper water by casting toward the middle.

Hearing a splash, I snapped my head to the left and watched someone in a boat playing a good-sized fish. I heard him yell, "A cutthroat. It's a good one!"

A few minutes later he held it up in the air and then released it. I thought it might have reached 20 inches. In this lake, regardless of size, all the fish must be returned to the water. I noted that he was on the shaded side. Because of the cold water, I had decided the trout would be warming their bodies in the sun's rays which would eventually trigger them to actively feed on midges or crustaceans. In the summer, the opposite reasoning would be sensible.

I stuck with my system of casting into deep water and kicking toward the dam where the lake was at its deepest point, but nothing struck my flies. When I reached it, I knotted a big Woolly Bugger to my tippet and figured that the trout still remained in their "winter holes." After criss crossing the area several times and trying other fly patterns, I moved to the far shoreline where it was shaded.

I muttered, "47 degrees. Logic says the trout go where it's the warmest."

I glanced at the bright side of the lake which I just fished.

Shifting to the light intensity theory, I thought maybe the trout on this side avoided bright sunlight, but I recalled many occasions when I caught them on the sunny side when the water was cold.

"Too bad I can't ask a trout why it seems to behave oddly at times."

The man in the boat shouted again and now I hurried toward him to find out what he was doing. He returned the cutthroat just as I was in talking distance.

"What are they hitting?"

I kicked hard to keep the wind from bouncing me into his boat.

"Zug Bugs."

"Really? That's what I was using."

"It must be crawled dead-slow."

"Just exactly how I fished it."

"This must be the spot."

He grinned at me and showed no signs of relinquishing his "fish hole." I noted shoreline points and bends so I could find it later in the day or the next time I returned. I tubed toward the middle as I crawled a black nymph on the bottom. This end opposite the dam was shallower and I hoped the combination of shade and thin water was the answer for today. After several more fly changes, I didn't know what to think.

The boater remained at his spot and he caught several more cutthroat. I concluded the rainbows and browns were still lethargic. I had little experience with cutthroat, but I knew they tend to be active when other trout species were sluggish. I also knew that when brown trout were introduced here the cutthroat population decreased. The man catching them subdued them quickly giving me the impression that they weren't a hard fighter. Preferring trout that streak toward the middle, jump, and give me a hard time, I tried not to let him bother me.

The afternoon water temperature reached 51 degrees and my fingers were crossed that it was enough of a difference to make the trout active, but it wasn't. At the end of the day, I sat in the car and warmed up with soup as I tried to figure where to fish in the morning.

Rising at 9:00, I drove down to a 1,000-foot-high lake and fished its 56 degree water which is perfect for trout. Clementine Lake seemed to sprawl its many watery acres to eternity. Its unchanging terrain of high cliffsides didn't give me any clues where I'd find its big rainbows. I felt that if there was going to be an insect hatch it would be on the sunny side. Now at 10:30 a.m. I fished with a brown Woolly Worm. Although bait or spin anglers often rise early and do well, I seldom find fly fishing worthwhile until the sun rises and spreads its golden rays across the surface. The rays of the sun penetrating below the surface sometimes brings immediate activity from bugs and insects followed soon by the trout.

I cast toward edges where reeds merged with rocks, where two big rocks almost touched, where a small brush pile met a submerged pile of rocks, points, and indentations of the shoreline always hoping for something to guide me in the right direction. Frequently I find that fishing parallel with the lake's edge provides the best action on steep-banked lakes like this one.

Rocky reservoirs usually have crayfish but every time I tried such patterns and worked it in puffs and jerks on the lake bottom I remained fishless. Since crayfish usually stay under the rocks during the bright part of the day, perhaps trout don't feed on them until late-afternoon shadows creep onto the lake. Knowing the habits and habitat of the small aquatic organisms is more important than owning a hundred fly boxes. My experience with imitating insects and bugs found in lakes tells me that I only need to suggest the shape, color, and size of an insect. The most important thing is to duplicate the behavior of the insect in the water. Minnows seem to be more common in lakes that have a shallow shelf that extends a short ways into the lake and that may be why bucktails and streamers haven't been productive in steep-banked reservoirs like Clementine. But Woolly Worms do catch the bass, bluegill, and trout of these deep lakes with high cliffs as its shoreline. I think the effectiveness of Woolly Worms is proof positive that exact imitation is not necessary, *most of the time.* For the two or three days out of 10 when the trout are super-selective, to catch them, I better be ready with a good imitation.

Persistence is the key on a lake like Clementine. I rounded another point and finned alongside it as I now cast a black

Matuka streamer and crawled it on the bottom only occasionally giving it a quick jerk. I was almost surprised when a fish struck it. A moment later I brought in an eight-inch bluegill, my favorite panfish. Quickly I released it and moved on to another area looking for the four to six-pound rainbows that I was informed swim somewhere in this lake.

I saw another reedy section of shoreline ahead of me but it looked like all the other reed-lined edges I already fished so I wasn't terribly excited.

"A good spot for feeding trout," I thought when I found a shallow ledge of rocks near the reeds.

Then I heard the hum of a speedboat coming around a bend below me and a moment later it cruised by me sending a series of waves toward the shoreline and a moment later I bounced in his wake. When the waves flattened out, I worked the area hard with various nymphs but nothing hit.

I hurried to the other side before another boat came along. Just as I began to fish the shaded bank with a large wet brown hackle, another bass boat zipped by me. He waved and I returned the greeting. I wondered if he and his friend caught anything. Today was one of the few times I wished for a boat. Exploring a big reservoir would be easier and I could reach the "fishy" areas quicker.

In the shade, I noted a 53-degree reading but the difference of three degrees wasn't meaningful since water in the 50s was great for trout although they fed the most actively from 55 to 65. Above 68, they hid under rocks and in weedbeds and seldom bulged.

I continued fishing in every direction while thinking I probably would have done better in a valley lake where I was bound to catch at least a bunch of bluegill but my mind, as usual, was stuck on trout.

I still don't know why I didn't catch trout at the fish-for-fun lake or Clementine Lake, but if there weren't any mysteries I don't think I'd continue fly fishing with such persistence or joy.

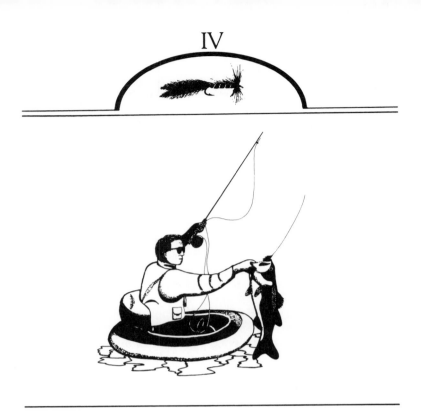

Choosing A Bass Lake

Most bass fishermen have a large variety of lakes to choose from when deciding where to fish. There are huge manmade reservoirs, natural rain-fed waters, sloughs off major rivers, stripmine lakes, highland lakes, and farm ponds of various sizes. The problem is made more complex deciding which bass species an angler likes best. Even how a bass fisherman enjoys his or her sport becomes a factor. In this chapter, I focus on float tubing, fly fishing, and largemouth bass.

A bass fisherman has less to worry about than a trout fly rodder since there usually is a limited altitude range for the basses in a given area and insect hatches aren't usually impor-

tant. Please note the word "usually." Bass do eat dragonfly and damselfly nymphs and other large insects, but such food
fare is secondary to minnows, crayfish, and frogs. The six factors that most affect a bass fisherman's choice of a lake are as
follows: lake configuration; amount of cover available; lake
size; depth of lake; type of lake; geographic area of lake.

These factors interrelate. A lake with a number of points,
coves, and arms tends to be large and a big lake is deep. A reservoir has a dam, inlet, outlet, and a riverbed whereas a pond is
likely to be shallow, round, and probably rain-fed. Bass in reservoirs normally grow faster and bigger than those in small waters
but are usually harder to find. Pond bass are not only easier to
find but also are more susceptible to fly fishing methods. My
brother-in-law, Ken Townsend, a canoeing enthusiast, and, like
me, mainly a fly fisherman, prefers the little places on farms
close to where he lives knowing his odds for huge bass (over
five pounds) are lower than if he concentrated on reservoirs. Big
bass can be caught from small waters but the smaller ones make
themselves more conspicuous and a devotee of the fly rod often
concentrates on bass from one to three pounds since they hang
close to the lake's edge and are fairly easy to catch and provide
an angler with a lot of action. Ken likes them because they
regularly hit popping bugs and the splashy take at the surface is
what makes him grin. In fact, I like that too! But, because I
know the feeling of trout to five pounds streaking out yards of
line, I probe the bottom with sinking lines for bigger fish. I'm
not strictly a lunker hunter. I mainly look for bass over two
pounds because they fight harder and have more stamina than
small ones. For these reasons, my lake preference is slightly different from Ken's. Because I am a tuber, I prefer mid-size (500 to
2,000 acre) reservoirs with a large range of cover and water no
deeper than 50 feet whereas Ken likes a small body of water no
more than 20 feet deep. Since he lives in Virginia and I live on
the West Coast, I suppose it's possible he's changed his mind
since we were last together but somehow I doubt it.

Setting fishing style aside, let's concentrate on the six factors
and become analytical. Configuration is listed first because I
believe it to be the most important. Regardless of the size,
depth, or type of lake, it isn't a good place to fish if the shoreline
is round and varies little with ground cover. Given a choice of a
500-acre lake which sprawls out and has many arms, coves, and

points or a 500-acre lake which is circular and is surrounded by low-lying brush, the first one is a better fish producer because it provides more shallow food-producing areas as well as deep-water sanctuaries where bass can hide from the rays of the sun (and anglers). With depths to 50 feet or more, bass roam at various levels throughout the year as the need occurs. Type of cover is next because bass hover near it. Logs, weeds, rocks, docks, brushpiles, undercut banks, and even sunken manmade objects like duck shanties or cars are all equal in a bass's sight. Always look for the maximum amount of hiding areas for a bass. I call lake configuration and availability of cover the constant factors. Regardless of how you fish or what time of year you fish, these two factors are important, but the last four, the variables, determine seasonable choices of where to fish.

The average angler starts fishing in April or maybe May. To have the best success early in the year, especially on flies, water temperatures should be above 60 – when bass become active. Shallow lakes (20 feet or less) which warm quicker than deep reservoirs are usually a better choice for April and May, but it is during these months when the water is often stained with mud after a hard rain. I know the feeling when you worked hard all week and looked forward to your first trip of the season but a thunderstorm blasted down with rain Friday night. Don't give up yet! Get out a map and find lakes in a geographic area that are hard rock, heavily forested, or higher in altitude than your own area. Such stillwaters are likely to be less roiled with mud. I realize not everybody has this opportunity, but it is easy to miss decent fishing possibilities by not researching every possible idea. Having lived in Missouri, Virginia, West Virginia, and Pennsylvania, I know there are mountainous regions with clear water lakes in all those states. Keep in mind, too, that often going up in altitude gives almost any angler the added bonus of catching rainbows and browns.

The type of lake, whether drainage or seepage, also influences the decision of where to fish. Despite its size, the seepage, or rain-filled lake warms rapidly early in the year therefore they are a better choice than drainage lakes which have an inlet, outlet, and a river channel. The moving current of the channel takes more time to warm than other bodies of water. In summary, for spring fishing look for small lakes, (under 1,000 acres – not 500, bass lakes average bigger than mountain trout lakes) shallow water, (less than 20 feet) seepage lakes, and impoundments in geographic areas less prone to become muddy.

In most of the country, spring and summer battle with each other for a long time before summer is finally victorious. In most places, spring occurs when air temperatures stabilize near 70 and summer when the temperatures stay above 80. Although May can be like spring or summer, I think of June through August as the hot (and muggy) season. The big reservoirs are usually at their best in early summer. The best choice for fly fishing during the warm months are stillwaters in foothill regions or farm ponds. Late July and August are tough almost anywhere, but I think reservoirs conjure up the hardest (and most futile) fly fishing that could ever exist. The best thing in July and August is to head into the mountains and fish for trout, however, the dedicated bass fly rodder who sticks to the larger farm ponds with depths to 40 feet is going to do well. His odds are increased if he finds such places with an inlet and outlet since current running through a lake keeps it a bit cooler than a rain-fed one. Any bass water with high trees or shrubbery alongside it is also a good choice, such cover provides protection from the sun. Night fishing is fine for boat anglers or bank fishermen, but I don't recommend it to float tubers. When I lived in Arizona, I constantly went to Becker Lake and thought I knew it as well as my apartment. I knew a tuber who told me where and how to fish it at night. He caught lunker trout most people only dream about and he tempted me to do likewise, but, one day, I kicked along the shoreline and I followed the bend toward the marina as I scanned the area for rising trout. At the last minute I noticed an underwater stump which I almost rammed my feet into. Startled, I turned away from it at the last minute. Here, on a lake I thought I knew well, was an underwater stump which I didn't know existed. Ever since then, I vowed never to tube at night.

September, in most bass fishing states, is the transition month toward fall. When the temperature sharply drops, the angler should be sitting in his or her tube! Now it doesn't matter where you fish. Bass, in most places, are feeding and attacking lures and flies as they gorge for the winter season but, when the feeding frenzy ends and before the first winter storm arrives, it becomes tough to catch bass, but as I remember Jason Lucas, a former fishing editor for *Sports Afield*, reporting, this is when an angler can catch the biggest bass of the season if you can withstand the cold. I have trout fished late in the season but my late-season bass fishing is limited. I don't know how to advise anyone on what type of lake to fish. If I were going to try it, my first thought would be to visit a small place known for big bass. If I didn't know any, I'd fish a big reservoir.

Warm weather winter bassin' exists in California, Arizona, and the Deep South and often it is a good time to fish. Most of the lakes in southern Arizona are big canyon reservoirs and require electronic gear but in the Deep South and in the Sacramento Valley, there are shallow lakes conducive to tubing and fly fishing. Now maybe you understand why I live in Sacramento!

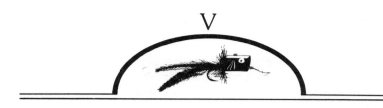

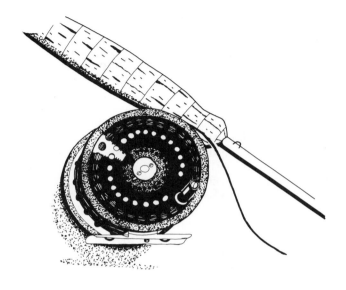

Float Tube Strategies

The high lakes of Arizona's White Mountains hold heavily muscled rainbows and browns up to 20 inches long. Over the course of numerous float tube outings to these lakes, I have caught more and more of these beautiful fish. My equipment, from the float tube to full-sinking lines of various densities, contributes greatly to my angling success, but just having the right gear doesn't insure that I will catch fish.

After five years of tubing in the White Mountain lakes and elsewhere, I've developed several strategies. Through the development of these tactics, my success has increased dramatically. These proven float tube methods and presentations can improve your lake fishing success.

I've discovered that the direction of the cast is crucial to float tube fishing success. Casting thoughtfully is more effective than a random series of casts. One day casting toward the shoreline with a number 16 Hare's Ear Nymph and inching it along the bottom can be the ticket, but on other days I must retrieve the fly from the middle of the lake toward the shoreline to catch fish. When neither of these approaches works, I find casting and retrieving parallel to the shoreline often brings strikes.

I seldom just troll a fly unless I'm kicking from one spot to another one on the opposite shoreline or at the other end of the lake. If a trout hits my fly enroute to a new place, I'm pleased, because I may have discovered a new area where trout congregate. By trolling a fly from one side of a lake to another, I frequently learn how trout group themselves together during a certain time of day or a particular season of the year.

Shooting tapers cast farther than full sinking lines, they facilitate line changes, and they save space in an already stuffed vest or float tube pocket. Although they offer these advantages, I prefer to use full sinking lines for several reasons. For close fishing (about 15 to 25 feet) in weed beds, I can make more accurate casts and softer presentations with a weight forward sinking line. A shooting taper combined with a nine-foot leader is usually about 40 feet long – more than I need in tight weed-bed situations. I use Scientific Anglers floating, fast, and extra-fast sinking lines, but Cortland sinking lines have similar sinking characteristics. The fishing principles apply to both brands of line. With the Scientific Anglers Wet Cel II (fast sinking) and the short cast technique, I can fish weedy shallows and also fish water as deep as 20 feet without changing spools or lines. When I need a longer retrieve in weed-beds, I use the second rod I take along rigged with a floating line. A Wet Cel III (Hi-D) line sinks my fly to almost 30 feet, so I don't need it in shallow water. I usually begin with the Wet Cel II and change only when I'm convinced the fish are in deeper water. Using a Wet Cel IV (Hi-Speed, Hi-D), I can plumb the depths of the big reservoirs near my home in Sacramento. A slow sinking line (Wet Cel I) does better in four to six-foot depths.

On long casts a floating (shooting) line and the connections between it and a shooting taper can interfere with sensitivity. A full sinking line provides a more direct line to my fly. I can usually feel my bucktail or Woolly Worm crawling over rocks, stumps, weeds, or smooth bottoms. That feel helps me determine what type of structure a lake bottom has, thus helping me make decisions on how to fish. Although often difficult to fish, underwater weed-beds hold insects and often actively feeding trout. Once I've located a weed-bed, I use a countdown technique to fish just above them. The technique is simple, if you know the sink rates of the sinking line you are using. For instance, the Wet Cel III (Hi-D) has a sink rate of from 3.25 inches to 4.25 inches per second. By counting the seconds on your watch, you can tell how deep the fly line has sunk. As an example, by waiting 10 seconds I know that my line is about 32 inches to 43 inches deep. When I find the depth where the fish are, I can simply use the same count repeatedly to reach that depth with my fly. I change the count to match each change of line.

Usually the fish are on the bottom or cruising in the shallows but seldom in the middle layers of the lake, therefore long retrieves that hold the fly on the bottom are important. When I'm fishing long casts, a full sinking line keeps my fly deeper, longer. When I make a cast from 25 to 65 feet, the line sinks to the bottom and acts like an anchor to keep my nymph there until I complete the retrieve and cast again. Yes, I often snag the lake bottom, but my line seldom gets entangled in brush, but most mountain lakes are relatively brush free.

When a decent hatch occurs and brings good fish to the surface, the feeding spree is usually short – perhaps 30 minutes. With a second rod and reel loaded with a floating line and strapped to my tube, I can change in seconds.

For most of my tubing I use a nine or 10-foot leader. After much experimentation, I've concluded that short (under six feet) leaders work well when I fish 25 feet or deeper with flies such as crayfish patterns that are presented most realistically when close to the bottom. I have fished successfully down to about 20 feet with longer leaders using small Woolly Worms and nymphs. Most of the time, I use 4X tippets because nearly all the lakes I fish are clear, allowing the fish a good view of the tippet.

Woolly Worms and soft fur nymphs are among the best flies for exploratory fishing. My favorite nymph patterns include the Hare's Ear Nymph, Gray Nymph, Zug Bug, and Beaver Nymph.

The brown and gray hackle wet flies combined with peacock herl or yellow floss are usually more productive than the standard feathered or winged wet patterns. I consider these hackle flies as nymphs. In spring I use number 12s and work down to number 16s in summer. In late summer and in fall, number 20 patterns fished near the surface do best for me. Brown, green, black, and gray Woolly Worms in numbers 8 to 12 consistently catch big trout. I like all-brown and all-black best, but I prefer dark and olive green or gray bodies mixed with brown hackle.

A note to fly tiers: Do not overdress your flies. Sparsely hackled flies work best. Although larger sizes are effective late in the year and in dirty water, I find that a number 12 Woolly Worm catches the most and biggest trout throughout the season.

When nymphs, hackle flies, and Woolly Worms fail, I dig out my box of bucktails. The box is loaded with Woolly Buggers in black and brown, Marabou Leeches and Matuka Streamers in the same shades and Muddler Minnows. Sizes 6 and 8 work well on my seven-weight rod.

When fishing unfamiliar lakes, I station myself far enough from the shoreline to have deep water both to my front and back. As I kick along, I begin by casting toward the bank. I seldom cast into grassy shorelines — except where they occur along sharp drop-offs or cliffs — because such thin water seldom holds good fish. I search for sharp edges, drop-offs that have relatively shallow water close to deeper water. To find such structure, I may need to kick farther out from the lake's contours. Often I see weeds disappear as the water deepens, creating a food-rich edge which trout like. They can chase after insects in the four-foot depths, and when finished dining, they can lazily fin back to the deeper water only a few feet away.

If a particular spot looks attractive, I turn my float tube to face it. Usually this positions me toward fishy-looking shoreline with a weed-bed or rocky point. I stay about 40 feet from the spot and fan-cast the entire area, usually beginning with the far left side and working clock-wise until I have covered all the water to the far right of the structure. If the water is deep, I make medium and long casts, but if it's only a few feet down to the bottom, I use short casts or switch to my second rod with the floating line. With a nine to 10-foot leader on the floating line, I have no trouble reaching the bottom with the fly. A five-weight outfit gives a softer presentation, but if you expect wind or to change from large to small patterns on the floating line, another seven-weight is better. In another chapter, I provide more details on the two-rod system.

When the line straightens out in front of you, continue kicking and keep retrieving the fly parallel with the bank and back toward you. It is easy to pick up four to six feet of line, false cast once or twice, and shoot the line coiled on the stripping apron. Check that the wind hasn't tangled the coils of fly line. Float tubes with a windbreak all around the angler help to keep the line in order. (I noticed this difference when I changed from the Mountain Top Trader basic model to the Buck's Bag Deluxe model that I now use.) Regardless of your float tube manufacturer and the angle of your cast, always allow the fly to sink to the bottom. When this fails to produce fish, try all levels between the bottom and surface.

I strive to constantly observe and experiment with my retrieves. I usually retrieve my fly with slow, even three-inch strips, pausing long enough to allow the line to drop onto the float tube apron between strips. I also vary the length and rhythm of my pulls — often within one long retrieve — a technique that prevents my falling into an unproductive, hypnotic cadence. The hand twist method also works well. It's done simply by twisting the line slowly around your line hand to create a measured, slow retrieve that simulates the natural swimming action of nymphs and crustaceans. Toward the end of a retrieve, I sometimes let the fly and line sink back toward the bottom before beginning a new retrieve. I remind myself that trout live in the water and not in trees or the air. It improves my fishing.

Most fly fishermen retrieve their flies too fast. My retrieves are often so slow that other anglers accuse me of trolling. Short even strips are best with Woolly Worms and nymphs, while longer and faster pulls work well with bucktails and streamers. Yet, I have also taken big trout by crawling bucktail and leech patterns. It always pays to try different things. You never know what will work unless you try it.

To effectively cover the shoreline as I kick along, I twist my body and cast farther behind me. Alternately casting toward the bank and away from it every 20 minutes or every 20 casts, I cover the shoreline well. I strive for my longest casts when sending the fly toward mid-lake. As I continue kicking along the shoreline, the fly line naturally curves back toward me until it is in a direct line with the float tube. Then I retrieve the line with strips and pauses. Frequently fish hit the fly just before the bend in the fly line straightens, perhaps because the action imparted by the straightening line and leader causes the fly to hop in a natural movement off the bottom.

Aquatic insects seldom swim in only one direction. To create a more realistic swimming action, I continually alter the direction of my rod tip during a retrieve.

When these two tactics fail, I make long casts straight ahead of me and swim the fly back as I keep finning parallel with the shoreline. The technique works most effectively in late summer with bucktails and streamers fished in lakes that have steep drop-offs.

I fish each fly pattern for 30 to 45 minutes, unless something works consistently, in which case I stay with it. One fly fished in many ways, at many depths, and near different kinds of structures (weeds, logs, rocks, inlets, outlets, and dams) results in higher yields than constantly changing flies. Confidence in the fly pattern and how it is being fished is of utmost importance. If I lose my optimism for the fly on the end of my leader, I immediately change to a new one.

Frequently fishing your favorite lake can help your success if you observe seasonable changes and daily fish movements, such as trout moving from one shoreline to another as the sun moves across the sky. I fished Rainbow Lake in Arizona using trial-and-error tactics until I learned the exact spots where trout lived. All day I kicked from one place to another. Once in a fishy-looking area, I cast until I covered the deep water by fishing toward midlake as well as the edge, and the shallows.

Apparently the trout in Rainbow Lake often faced one direction to feed on insects floating to them from that direction and later, cruised along the weed edges to catch insect hatches, and at other times reversed themselves to feed on bugs scuttling shoreward from deeper regions of the lake. Trout always take advantage of insect behavior. As an example, damselfly naiads swim away from the bank toward the outer rims of weed beds where the trout are waiting to prey upon them. Crayfish leave their rocky hideouts late in the day and head shoreward and become vulnerable to feeding trout. Water beetles dive up and down in the lake making themselves easy targets for hungry trout. The fish know these cycles and they follow them. With close observation, you can learn the aquatic food cycles of your lake and learn to fish to trout feeding on them.

Learning the seasonal movements of trout can also improve

your fishing. For instance, in spring trout usually forage closer to the shoreline to take advantage of the warmer shallow-water temperatures and the insect life those waters produce before the rest of the lake warms. In early spring, the shallows can provide excellent fishing.

Droughts often cause trout to stay deeper throughout much of the spring and summer. During summer days, they station themselves in deep spots adjacent to shallow, insect-rich weedy areas. As water levels lower, the trout usually roam a bit farther away from the weeds and close to river channels, if the lake has one.

In autumn, the weather greatly influences where the fish congregate. The best late-season fishing occurs when summer rains keep the lakes at peak levels. At such times big trout move close to the shoreline to gorge themselves before the lean months of winter arrive. In fall, low water can make for troublesome fishing. Weeds are often much thicker than in summer and restless trout seldom stay in one place. I find that casting parallel to the bank, trying various stripping retrieves, and kicking in a "S" pattern toward a section of shoreline often locates cruising fish.

Although high winds can make tubing difficult on most any lake, I continue to fish even while whitecapped waves of up to five feet splash around me. I don't spill over because most of my weight (which is considerable) is below the water's surface which makes tipping nearly impossible. If I alter my casting stroke, I can still fly cast fairly well on windy days. Sometimes I cast with the wind, but when I do, I turn away from the fly line, angle into the wind, and furiously kick to keep from being blown into my sinking line. To cast into the wind, I snap my rod back sharply and keep my backcast high. But in a strong wind, the sinking fly line can quickly blow toward me where it can create a mess around my legs! The best bet is to cast toward the shore, angle my cast up or down-wind, and kick away from the line. During the summer, wind revitalizes lethargic trout and that is why I continue fishing under such harsh conditions.

Lake fishing from a float tube can be enjoyable and rewarding, but it isn't easy. Wind and weather can make the going tough, but sticking with a solid plan and proven tactics can put the odds in your favor. If you are willing to develop a system of tackle and techniques suited to your own lakes, you can increase your chances of success during each outing. Using a proven plan for lake fishing can lead to productive days that result in many fish hooked and landed. One of my recent trips ended in a 25-fish day with a number of browns and rainbows in the 16 to 18-inch class. Fine tune your float tube strategies and you can also enjoy the same kind of results.

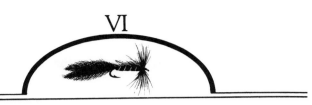

VI

Your Watch Is A Fishing Tool

How long should your dry fly, nymph, wet fly, bucktail, or streamer soak in the water? One fellow tuber told me 15 minutes was sufficient. He represents the extreme theory that trout are totally selective and hit only one size, color, and type of fly. At the other extreme, I have met older gentlemen who were loyal to only half a dozen patterns and rarely tied on other flies. Both the presentationist and imitationist have their good days. Frequently, they both catch trout at the same time and may only be a few yards apart! I can easily recall when, as a beginner, such things confused me and I didn't know what to believe. My own system is a compromise and I have confidence in it. Confidence is the key word in the previous sentence. Without it, a person is lost and won't succeed at anything. But this faith must be founded not only on facts but also an organized plan of attack. Because of the work done by angling entomologists like Schwiebert, LaFontaine, Hughes, and many others, we know what patterns resemble an insect order or species. In fact, these scientific writers support the presentation theory when they disclose to laymen how these insects swim in the water and where they live. Their books give us the facts which build our confidence in the flies we tie on our leaders. Now all we need is a sense of order for using these flies. In another chapter, I show how a tuber can correlate his knowledge of entomology with his knowledge of a specific lake and how such thinking helps to fish a pattern in the right section of a lake.

For the moment, let's concentrate on an effective way to utilize fishing time on our favorite lake. It is easy and effective. The only thing you need is your wristwatch.

The best way to tell about it is through example. Here's how it worked for me on a recent trip to a fish-for-fun lake in the Sierra Nevada Mountains:

I approached this popular little lake and observed a 16-inch brown trout cruising in the shallows. Even after scrutinizing the surface film, studying the rocky bottom, and turning over a few rocks, I only noticed a tiny gnat hovering above the surface, but the splashing of other trout indicated they weren't feeding on midges. Once in my float tube, I tried to fool them with a number 16 wet Black Gnat thinking that the color was correct and hoping the larger size would appeal to the trout. I had fished it about 20 minutes and contemplated a change, but a breeze came down from the peaks and it wrinkled the lake's surface and ended the shallow feeding of those browns.

With my Orvis All-Rounder in my hands and the Far and Fine outfit under tube straps, I probed the bottom with a Wet Cel II sinking line. I began to fish the near bank with a number 8 brown Woolly Worm but when I did I checked the time — 12:00 noon. Using my usual slow/even strip, I worked the deep water, edges, and shallow areas by casting toward, away, and parallel with the bank. I also roamed the middle near the river channel and away from it. After covering rocky and weedy shorelines and using super-slow retrieves to high-speed strips of the line, I glanced at my watch and noted 40 minutes had passed. I tied on a number 16 Black Nymph to the 4X tippet and 40 minutes later switched to a number 16 gray-hackle yellow body wet fly. After these changes, it became obvious the trout didn't like this end of the lake today.

The half hour with the wet pattern lasted until 2:00 p.m. As I finned toward the other end of this 70-acre lake, I fished with a number 12 Gray Nymph. Following the contours of the shoreline opposite my wagon, I continually cast in every direction, at all depths and with many different retrieves. Until it's a habit, make a point to change direction every 20 casts and to employ a new retrieve on every sixth cast. Confidently, I fished my way to the weedy end of the lake, but when I reached it 35 minutes later, I changed to a number 12 Hare's Ear Nymph which I cast to the edges of the weed beds, the open pockets between them, and nearby open water. Despite all my efforts, not one trout struck my fly, yet I retained my optimism since I not only knew there were lunker trout in the lake but I also had faith in my fishing strategies.

An hour passed. It was the longest period of time that I spent with one pattern.

Late afternoon arrived and the wind grew colder and stronger.

"Typical for November," I muttered as I tightened the jacket hood around my neck and face. Seldom finding early morning fishing good, particularly late in the season, I began late in the morning.

Forty-seven degree water nipped at my lower legs which were wrapped in neoprene and polypro underwear. Although I was tired of the wind, I intended, one way or another, to catch at least one decent trout.

Almost seeing my breath, I changed to a number 12 Zug Bug. At about 4:00 p.m. I industriously fished it as I went through the various line strips and depths near the weeds. On the twentieth cast, I sent the Zug Bug to a clump of weeds. An inch at a time, I pulled it at a pace faster than a crawl but not quite a medium speed. A fish hit it and I struck with my line finger and rod tip. After pressuring the trout away from the weeds, the battle was waged in deeper, but "safer" water. Soon, I released a thick 16-inch brown probably weighing about two pounds. I've noticed most lake brown trout are thicker and heavier than a stream brown of the same length.

I rested briefly and talked with another tuber who told me

of a morning midge hatch which brought up four-pound trout. I decided such a hatch in November was unusual. At least that was what I wanted to believe. Briefly, I wished I had arrived sooner, but I also knew that until the sun beamed its rays on the water the air must have been under 40 degrees. That's too cold for me!

Near 5:00 p.m., the skies darkened. Cold, hungry, and tired, I reluctantly headed for the car. Not wanting to mess with finicky leader tippets in the wind, I left the Zug Bug on the end of my leader.

During the six hours I spent on the lake, I used seven flies. I used each fly about 45 minutes which I consider about right. In that time I could determine both where to find the trout and the effective depth and retrieve. If I hadn't used my watch, I might have fished one pattern longer than necessary. I could remember when I was too loyal to favorite patterns. When I began using my watch, I not only became a more thoughtful angler but also caught more fish. Remember, your watch is a fishing tool!

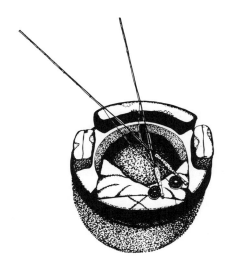

VII

Two Rods Are Better Than One

To my right and close to shore a trout jumped. It's splash startled me from a reverie and I was surprised at the size of the ring it made.

It rose again but several feet away from where I first saw it smack the surface. Despite the Wet Cel II line, I cast my Hare's Ear nymph toward it, kept the rod tip up, and stripped the fly as it hit the surface, but the trout wanted nothing to do with my nymph scooting across the lake's surface. Sometimes I caught rising trout with that tactic, but I learned that the high rod, fast strip technique, and sinking line was, at best, a compromise.

The trout only came up twice and then stayed under. Where the trout went was anybody's guess. But another trout rose close to the bank and I tubed toward the shoreline to see if a hatch was in progress. I noticed only a few gnats hovering above the waterline near the grassy edge of Arizona's Rainbow Lake. Another trout splashed. I had just switched to a floating line. As I reeled in the sinking line, snipped off the fly, spooled it on the reel, and snapped a new one on my Battenkill IV Orvis, a number of trout rose all around me. They continued to distract me as I tried to string leader and line through all the guides of my Orvis All-Rounder which is eight-feet, three inches long. As I fumbled with 4X tippet and a wet fly, I glanced around thinking now there were less trout rising around me. By the time I was ready to fish, the rising trout were back on the lake's bottom. I sat still for maybe five minutes hoping for another rise, but the lake had gone dead, like it was before the trout suddenly appeared. To respool the other line back on seemed silly.

"Perhaps," I thought, "there are a few trout on the opposite shoreline and in the weed beds."

I crossed over quickly and fished the shallows with much determination, but nothing hit the various nymphs and bucktails I tried.

I spent the next 15 minutes returning to the sinking line. An hour passed and afternoon shadows crept onto the lake. I was tempted to fish in the four-foot depths where the shadows lingered, but I knew that would mean I'd have to switch back to the floating line.

Too many times I've been through the ritual of spooling and respooling lines onto my reel and I decided there had to be a better way. I knew shooting tapers were an alternative, but, because I had several fly rods, another idea occurred to me and, since this plan of action didn't involve money, I had to try it first.

My two-rod system worked perfectly the first time I tried it about five years ago and I wondered why I didn't think of it sooner. Instantly, I could go from a sinking line to a floating one when situations demanded a different approach. It is quicker to unstrap a rod than to re-loop and uncoil a shooting taper. Hatches on a lake are not only rare but often quite brief, therefore one must be able to quickly change from one type of tackle to another. Even during the time it takes to change a shooting taper, a hatch can be over.

Perhaps you would tell me, "I like to use weighted flies on a long leader. All I need to do is change flies."

A few hours previous to a hatch your method works well. However, for most of the day, the damsel fly naiads, caddis larvae, mayfly nymphs, and the tiny members of the Diptera family stay on the bottom, either resting on rocks, logs, weeds, or crawling up and over such structure. As soon as you begin to retrieve your weighted fly, it jumps up from the bottom. Hatches cannot be predicted to a precise moment. For this reason, the fly fisherman must fish right on the bottom until the magic hour is made obvious to the angler.

Another good reason for staying with the sinking line is that not only do the insects stay near the bottom, but minnows, crayfish, scuds, and snails also hug the bottom, or the cover on it. Almost any fly type is more effective on a sinking line, but when it is time to work flies on a floating line, in order to cash in on the hatch, a quick change is necessary.

The biggest problem to solve when using the two-rod system is deciding which two outfits to take and which two flies to tie on the leaders. The answer is simple for those who also like to spin fish, but for the dedicated fly rodder the solution is more complex, particularly if he fishes for all kinds of fish under many different circumstances.

The main factors to consider when rigging up two rods are: weather conditions, size of the lake, type and size of the fish most common in the lake to be fished, and the size of the flies to be cast.

The lakes of Arizona's White Mountains, where I learned most of my trout lake fishing, are notorious for winds. If I were to quit fishing every time the wind was strong, I'd hardly fish. With two seven-weight rods — an Orvis All-Rounder and a Cortland 8½-foot model — I can not only handle the wind but also cast flies from size 4 to 20 which allows me to catch most of the common freshwater fish. When I fish in small places or I need a delicate presentation, my second rod is an Orvis Far and Fine, a seven-foot, nine-inch rod for five-weight line, but a six and seven-weight combination also works well. I recommend the six-weight rod for the floating line and the seven-weight outfit for the sinking line. A seven and a eight or nine-weight combination is better if trophy fish and big reservoirs are the main target. At the other extreme, a five and six-weight rod duo is excellent for small alpine lakes at high elevations. Because wind can always be a problem on any reservoir, rods should be at least eight feet long.

For all-round use, fast and extra fast sinking lines are the most useful. On lakes with steep banks which provide minimum shallow food shelves and weed-beds, I thought of rigging both rods with sinking lines of different sink rates since good game fish are usually deep, but on the whole, a floating-sinking set-up is better. The fast sinking line (Wet Cel II) is at its best in lakes whose depth don't exceed much beyond 25 feet. To quickly reach 35-foot depths, Wet Cel III line does better. Super fast sinking lines are available for the biggest and deepest of lakes. I only use the Scientific Angler's line as one example. There are other companies with excellent lines, but to be consistent and well-organized, it is best to stay with the same manufacturer in order to not overlap the sink rate of your lines. In order to have great flexibility for fishing methods, I rig my Wet Cel II and III differently. With a nine-foot 4X leader on the Wet Cel II, I can quietly present a small nymph and fish it just above the weed beds. I attached a 2X, six-foot leader to the Wet Cel III line and this allows me to fish a big fly right on the bottom of a deep lake. If I need stronger tippets for snags or big fish, it is easy to cut back on the leader. I start with 2X and 4X tippets because they bring me more strikes than heavier ones. I find this equally true of bass.

I seldom use dry flies since few daytime hatches are long or intense enough to entice good-sized trout off the bottom. I'm not a lunker hunter, but I do prefer trout over a foot. The main exception might be the first two hours of the day but I'm too much of a night owl to check it out!

The main daytime hatches I encounter on lakes are the damsel flies, *Callibaetis* mayflies, midges, and small caddis flies. The underwater form is the most important with these insect orders. The damsel fly naiads vary from green to light tan but brown dominates. The best hook sizes are from 10 to 12. Depending on altitude, they hatch in late May to August. The *Callibaetis*, or brown drake, a May through July insect, is imitated best on hooks from 12 to 16 whereas the caddis flies range from number 16 to 22. They vary from brown to gray and pop off the surface anytime from May to October. For the damsel fly, sparsely-tied Woolly Worm's or Hare's Ear nymphs are effective. For super-selective fish, exact imitations like the ones Dave Whitlock or Hal Janssen tie are necessary. They also tie an exact imitation of the *Callibaetis* nymph, but, most of the time, I stick with a Hare's Ear Nymph for it. Midge pupae and small wet hackles do a good job on midge hatches. Black is the most common, but I have become aware of red, yellow, and gray pupaes. I have yet to find a caddis pattern that worked well. I continue to experiment, but I have been surprised how well standard number 16 wet flies work. In a later chapter, I elucidate upon this idea.

A dry fly is necessary for the flying ant "hatch" or when a large number of grasshoppers land on the water. However, neither can be predicted to a time of day. I have yet to experience a "grasshopper fall" and usually the flying ant surprises me. It is the only hatch I've experienced which provides good dry fly action. Since it is a large insect (number 10 and 12), I was quite amazed the first time I encountered it. It was only my second season in Arizona and in the West. My "eastern" mentality had me thinking mayfly or caddis until I lowered my face close to the waterline. By the time I straightened up in the tube and tied on the proper fly, the "hatch" ended.

Correlating this entomology with the use of two rods is fairly simple. Dark and gray winged wet flies like the Dark Cahill, Leadwing Coachman, Hare's Ear, and Black Gnat in size 16 on the floating line combined with an appropriate nymph on the sinking line provides the versatility needed during the daytime hatches.

Fly tiers take note: The Hare's Ear nymph and other fur bodied flies dressed in a slim taper, a sparse body, and without the gold ribbing or lead perform much better than the standard dressing. Consistently it outfishes the ribbed full-bodied nymph, throughout the year, but most dramatically during a strong damsel-fly hatch.

Other nymphs which work effectively from spring to fall are the Zug Bug, Gray, Beaver, American March Brown, olive Hare's Ear, and the black Hare's Ear.

A wide variety of Woolly Worms give the angler good flexibility for imitating underwater bugs. All-brown, all-black, tan-brown hackle, and yellow-brown hackle are effective in sizes from eight to twelve. Larger sizes seem better in fall or in heavily-roiled water, but nearly 98 percent of the time the size 12 catches most of my fish throughout the year and many of them weight up to five pounds. I also find that size 8 works better than larger patterns when fishing hard-fished bass lakes.

Some of the bass I've hooked have been around six pounds.

Large portions of a day on a mountain lake or a bass reservoir are devoid of any insect activity therefore Woolly Worm and bucktail or streamer combinations are worthwhile when using two rods. Remember to curve about in the water when you tube. Insects, bugs, leeches, crustaceans, and minnows seldom swim in smooth motions or in straight lines.

For bass fishermen, the four best set-ups beginning with the sinking line are: Woolly Worm-bucktail, bucktail-Woolly Worm, bucktail-popping bug, and Woolly Worm-popping bug. For trout anglers, the good combinations are: nymph-nymph, Woolly Worm-nymph, Woolly Worm-wet fly, nymph-wet fly, bucktail-nymph, nymph-bucktail, and Woolly Worm-bucktail.

One can easily go overboard choosing bucktails and streamers. The Muddler Minnow, black and brown Woolly Buggers, brown and green Marabou bucktails, and brown and black Matukas from number 4 to 10 cover a lot of territory. When bass fishing, flashier shades are also useful.

Most of the time, the rod under the straps is not in my way. It helps to point it away from the shoreline. When playing a fish, swiveling around keeps a large fish away from the second rod. For tubers who weave in and out of a forest of trees, the strapped rod could be rigged up and broken down into sections. (For two-piece rods only!)

The extreme versatility of the second rod is most noticeable when the angler works a section of shoreline with the sinking line and then returns to the starting point and switches to the floating line. Often this change results in fish otherwise uncaught.

In the coldest part of spring and autumn when trout invariably hug the bottom I stick with one rod and the sinking line, but for the bulk of the year, the second rod is more than handy. It is indispensable!

VIII

The Seasonable Tuber

There are two approaches to lake fishing: first, to pick a lake where fish are actively feeding for any given time of year or; second, to fish and learn one lake well regardless of the time of year. Chapters two through four are to help the angler who enjoys the first approach. When a fisherman falls under the spell of a particular lake, he or she (like I have) becomes obsessed with fishing it throughout the year and accepts the challenge to fish it when the trout are not actively moving. In this chapter, I hope to help those who prefer to fish one (or two) favorite lakes most of the time.

After a number of years learning a few lakes well, I developed some generalities about trout behavior which can be applied to most other stillwaters that hold cold water fish. The accompanying diagram (figure 3) reveals some trout behaviors which are important to know. Although trout have the same instincts and actions in lakes across the United States, the lakes differ with the particular insect, bug, or minnow which needs to be imitated and the different type of cover available to the fish. The typical trout fisherman usually fishes in the mountains therefore I am focusing this chapter on that subject. As a Californian, I define mountain lakes as those at 5,000 feet and higher. Lakes down to 1,000 feet are foothill and below 1,000 feet are valley lakes. I break the season into spring, summer, and fall. Here in California, winter trout fishing is possible since many of the deep valley reservoirs hold trout but my emphasis for this chapter and book is on the typical fishing months. The seasons — spring, summer and fall — need to be clarified since it is important to the understanding of how a "seasonable tuber" fishes. For me, spring is when the air stabilizes near 70 degrees and the water is close to 55 degrees. In summer, the air remains at 80 or above and the water is close to 60. Fall arrives when air temperatures return to 60 and the water hovers near 50. Although the following methods and observations are universal, the insect hatches I write of are reflective of Arizona's White Mountains and the Sierra Nevada waters east of Sacramento.

Seasonable Movements Of Trout

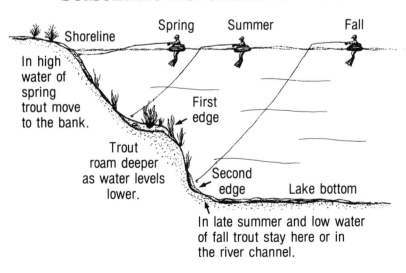

SPRING

Before spring has completely arrived, there is an in-between period as the water warms. The trout haven't quite shaken the doldrums of winter from their system yet; they're beginning to move away from the deep holes. It's difficult to pin this time of year down, but I suspect that on those days when the air is first becoming comfortable yet the nights are bone-chilling cold represents this "gray" in-between period. It is a frustrating time to fish and can last longer than I like. One minute, in the morning, I might pick up a trout as I cast inward toward the bank but my next strike is near noon and down deep. The best thing, I think, is to stay deep and keep the flies near the lake bed and occasionally cast toward the side of the lake. During this early spring period, retrieves parallel with the bank are likely to bring the most hits which are usually light bumps often difficult to detect. Concentrate on where the line cuts through the water and watch for side movements.

Finally spring arrives. The sun beams down and the trees are budding new leaves (unless they're evergreens!) but the best sign of the new fishing season is a certain hatch — men and women in boats, tubes, and on the bank! Often, the water is high and maybe slightly roily. In mountain lakes, especially those with hard or rocky bottoms, the water usually stays clear. The fish have moved close to the shoreline often just above the first edge where the lake bottom dips toward deep water. It usually is best to station the tube about 15 feet from the edge and to cast to the shoreline. If the water is unusually high and the sides of the lake are at least four feet deep, it is good to cast right to the grass or weeds since the trout may hug the cover and have enough depth for security. Fan casting helps find them, but in any kind of high water condition, the casts should be placed within a few feet of each other since it is still too early for them to roam far from where they are resting or feeding.

The theory often employed for spring fishing — highly visible patterns — is correct if the water is dirty, but from discussions with anglers and comparing results, I think fly fishermen exaggerate the point when they use sizes larger than six and fish with bright reds, oranges, pinks, and other such shades. On the whole, such patterns are better for bass. When I first began lake fishing in Arizona on Becker Lake, I fished too much with bucktails like Mickey Finns, red and white patterns, yellow marabous, and black marabous, all of which were large and

51

over-dressed. I was constantly outfished by the those who used nymphs. Finally I got smart and tied on a number 10 Gray Nymph. Not many casts later, I had a strike. It was my first fish on a barbless hook and I lost it, but soon, with the same nymph, another trout hit and I landed it. Yet the water was roily and that trip and other spring outings proved to me that number 10 and 12 nymphs were the most effective. The four patterns that have been the most effective early in the year are the Gray Nymph, Zug Bug, black Hare's Ear, and black Woolly Worm. They work best cast toward the sides of the lake and crawled on the bottom but, as I wrote in the chapter on float tube strategies, it is always good to alter the direction of the cast from parallel, to shoreward and vice versa on a regular basis. What I'm stressing to seasonable tubers is what generally works at a given time of year.

In spring, the most consistent insect activity comes from evening hatches of midges. Frequently, I notice anglers heading back to cars when darkness first settles on the horizon. Since, often throughout the year, evening brings trout to the surface, such behavior of fishermen mystifies me. I recall the first time I witnessed a good midge hatch. I was with Al Williams, fellow member of the Desert Fly Casters in Mesa, Arizona. The wind calmed leaving a metallic sheen on the lake's surface. We moved the boat closer to the weedy shoreline and waited for something to happen. We had a very sure feeling that a change was in the process. All day the trout refused to budge from the depths and strike our flies. We could almost feel it in the air — a crispness, the abrupt calming of the wind, and a silence that is similar to one that prefaces a storm.

Then I heard a slurping sound and I darted my head up from my fly box. Another fish rose and soon more rises followed. My fingers suddenly fumbled trying to do what they did easily all day. I dropped the wet fly and reached for a black midge pupa but the number 20 fly seemed to take forever to tie on the leader.

Finally I cast to a riser but the trout didn't like my imitation. "Now what do I do?" I thought to myself.

"Cast to the rainbow to the right of your fly, you dummy!"

After answering my own question, I lifted the line and cast toward it and lightly twitched the line.

The line tightened. He got it! Oops, it jumped and threw the fly back at me. Momentary depression became excitement when several other trout rose almost in the same spot. I cast toward one of them and hoped the big one would find my fly first. My rod tip dipped. I brought it up and the glass fibers stretched into an arch as a trout sent vibrations down to the cork grip. Handling it more carefully, I soon brought the fish my way. It wasn't the big one, yet for my first midge-caught trout, I thought it respectable at 15 inches. The heavily-muscled rainbow was probably close to two pounds. Typically, the hatch was brief but intense. It ended as quickly as it started when the last daylight succumbed to the growing darkness.

Always fish during the last hour of the evening. A dull day can end dramatically. The Becker lake midge hatch proved to be like most spring hatches. The Diptera species was black, required a number 20 pattern, and it hatched late in the day. It is the only good hatch that I've experienced on lakes early in the year. Most years spring is April through May.

SUMMER

Again, there is a nebulous period between spring and summer but it is not only less frustrating to fly fishers but it is also short lived. Remember, water warms and cools slower than air. When summer predominates, the water temperatures are spring-like to the trout. As the water warms, the lake returns to normal or slightly below normal water levels and the trout respond by leaving the shoreline and moving to the "lip," the area just under the edge. Here, it is easy for them to feed on insects and minnows. With water temperatures rising from 55, the trout are more active and feed with more regularity. At 60, the *Callibaetis* mayfly and the damsel fly naiad bring big trout toward the surface. I was amazed and frustrated the first time I experienced the latter.

I was tubing Arizona's Rainbow Lake. Even at 9:00 a.m. in early June, the sun beamed toward the earth and quickly warmed the air. An array of small insects hatched but only the bluegill and small trout (under a foot) rose for them. Desiring the three, four, and five-pound trout the lake held, I stayed on the bottom with my Wet Cel II line and various nymphs and Woolly Worms picking up an occasional bluegill. As morning ticked toward noon, I suddenly saw small creatures wriggling in the water.

"Almost like a tadpole," I thought almost out loud, "but they seem too small for that."

They swatted their little "tail-like" fins back and forth in the water and soon crawled onto the tube.

"Funny-looking buggers," I said.

Two boys in a boat turned around as if they heard me. Glancing away from them, I smiled and thought that the only problem with tubing by myself was the tendency to talk to my fly rod every now and then. If I followed the rule of never tubing alone, I'd seldom fish. Being single and with friends who either didn't tube or who didn't fish made me a solitary tuber, but loneliness was impossible when my mind was always filled with thoughts. Like right now, as I lifted one of those "tadpole-like" creatures onto a finger and scrutinized it, I was perplexed as I tried to identify it.

A big trout smacked the surface startling me. When I darted my head up and looked toward the rise, I noticed the damsel flies flitting above the water line and I made the connection between it and the larva on my finger.

With the sinking line I cast toward it. Sometimes this natural impulse combined with a high rod tip and a fast retrieve worked, but, just now, it failed as other rainbows rose all around me. Because I couldn't be sure if they were actually feeding on top or underneath the surface, I stayed with the sinking line and tried various flies. After switching to my floating line, I cast a Hare's Ear nymph toward the bank, and brought it back in even, medium strips; a trout struck and cartwheeled in the air. Heavy surges throbbed throughout the length of the Orvis All-Rounder as the rainbow sizzled out line and headed for the middle of the lake. Playing tug-of-war, first I gained line, then the trout did. I hadn't felt such strength since I fished Yellow Breeches Creek in Pennsylvania, but this time I landed the trout. It wasn't as big as I expected the rainbow to be. The 16-inch trout had wide flanks and I admired its beauty before releasing it.

I went on to catch almost 30 trout that day. Most were rainbows and a few reached 18 inches. I determined that the Hare's Ear nymph and brown Woolly Worm did best that day. At home, I verified that the "wriggly thing" was the naiad of the damsel fly. If I had to fish only one hatch of the year, I'd go for this one because the hatch usually lasts all day. After fishing the damsel hatch for five years, I learned to use the sinking line prior to the ascent of the naiad but to switch to the floating line as soon as the naiads were in the surface film. Water temperature is the key. The "pre-hatch" period occurs from about 58 to 62 degrees. I always cast toward the weeds and bring the imitation back toward me in even moderate strips. I also discovered that to cover the complete cycle effectively I should start fishing with green patterns as the water approached 60 when the naiads were on the bottom. They changed to brown later in the season or later in the hatch and to be successful I had to change the color of my Woolly Worm. As the last generations of damselflies arrived, they became tan in color. It was a challenge to ascend and descend to lakes of different altitudes to continue fishing this hatch at peak levels.

The *Callibaetis* mayfly is also excellent but I never found it to be as strong as the damselfly hatch. The same flies work for both insects. When the *Callibaetis* neared toward an end, summer definitely arrived. The damselfly hatch frequently continued through September, but it slacked off in August.

Trout move deeper as the water levels lower but they seem to hug the downward slope of the shoreline, therefore the most effective cast is still inward. When a hatch isn't in process, the nymphs (or wets) that caught summer trout are the number 16 brown hackle, (peacock body), Beaver Nymph, Hare's Ear nymph, number 12 yellow-brown hackle Woolly Worm and all-black Woolly Worm. They nearly always worked the best when they were crawled on the bottom.

By stationing the tube about 50 to 60 feet from the side of the lake, I cast toward it but dropped the fly in the water just above the edge and retrieve it along the bottom contours. Late in the afternoon, sometimes the opposite approach was better.

The worst time of the year, for me anyway, is August and much of September. As a "seasonable tuber," the best thing to do is to fish the river channel, springs, deep water near feeder creeks, or near the dam which usually provides the deepest (and coolest) water in the lake. It is a good idea to learn how deep these spots are so the right line is used. When I added the Wet Cel III to my system, I was able to fish down to 30-foot depths. With the two sinking lines, effectively fishing most areas is possible. If I couldn't feel bottom with the Wet Cel II, I changed to the faster sinker. The lake's contours often helped me choose which line to use. Gradual slopes meant I stuck with the Wet Cel II. Cliffsides jutting deeply into the reservoir told me to use the other line. Yet, I'd probably buy a handheld depth finder if someone manufactured one. That way I'd know the exact depth.

FALL

It begins as early as mid-September or as late as November, but on the average, October is definitely fall. In fact, October is my favorite month to fish. The mountain air is crisp and the water hovers in the mid 50s. Trout are active and in search of food. It is either the most exciting time of the year for lake fishing or the worst. It all depends on the weather.

If the lakes remained full of water throughout the year, the trout migrate close to the bank and fishing is almost identical to spring, but if a lake continued to shrink, in most cases, the trout remain in deep water and are subject to strange mood swings. At least, that's the way it seems.

In high water conditions, I face the shoreline and cast toward it, but in low water situations, I generally work the deep water and circle around the bank at the point where the side contour of the lake meets the bottom. I call this intersection the "second" edge. (Look again at figure 3) The ultimate way to find it is with a depth finder, but such equipment is bulky and probably unnecessary. Cast inward and feel the fly bump on the bottom. Kick away from the shoreline until the line is sunk in a straight line. Move forward and fish just above where the line straightened. This is the "second edge" which often is where trout locate themselves in late summer.

The one hatch I've encountered late in the year is a micro-caddis but it usually isn't intense and therefore doesn't affect the large trout. If they aren't hitting, the day can be saved by imitating the hatch with number 20 or 22 brown or gray Bivisibles or Elk-Hair Caddises. Most of the time, though, I stick with the sinking line and work small nymphs, Woolly Worms, or wets from top to bottom. Winged wet flies on the floating line often fool rising trout. The Adams is among the best patterns for such fishing.

When there is no sign of insect activity, I alternate between Woolly Worms, bucktails, and nymphs. My retrieve is usually dead slow. Two of the best colors are black and dark green with brown hackles. I like sizes 6 and 8 but, as the season approaches winter, the larger sizes seem more effective. Zug Bugs probably rate as the best nymph for late in the season, but the Hare's Ear and hackled wet flies like the Brown Hackle (peacock body) also work well. Matukas and Woolly Buggers are standards for this time of year.

When the trout finish their feeding frenzy, they cozy up to

cover somewhere on the bottom. The biggest ones, I think, find a place close to the river channel or close to the most choice form of underwater cover. Trout don't school although they often congregate together. Each one is different. Except for small ones, bass are the same way. This change in behavior is abrupt and usually takes me by surprise. I always aim to fish frequently in October and, when I know the lake, I do well. The weather is comfortably cool unless a wind rises. Ducks and birds accompany me and fill the air with chirps or quacks and remind me that there is no such thing as a lonely angler. Often, in farmland areas, the leaves of the surrounding forest show off an array of oranges, yellows, and browns. Squirrels and other small animals scamper about the edges of the lake and woods. Sometimes, a hawk soars high above me or a loon pokes a beak into the shallow areas of the lake. But then, there is that day in November when the tree branches are naked and the forest is silent. I know the end of the season is upon me. The lake spreads out as flat as a desert and a gray sky foretells snow. Persistence and deep fishing is the key but I also think of catching the biggest trout of the season on that final day of the year. I don't think the fly matters much. The great big bucktails, they say, are the best but I have yet to prove it. The few trout I net late in November are browns of average size and they hit nymphs like the Zug Bug or Hare's Ear.

One time, as I tubed Rainbow Lake in late November, I circled around a bend in the shoreline and lifted my head toward the sky. Peering into the lake as I searched for bugs, insects, or minnows, I stared at the spot where my fly line sliced into the water — to get an imaginary fix on where my fly might be and how it looked when I stripped and jerked on the line.

When I looked skyward, I suddenly became aware of something tiny and whitish swirling about in the wind. I sighed and, at noon, a plume of gray air left my nose.

"What is that?" I wondered.

I cast toward mid-lake, hooked a brown, and soon relieved it from the sting of the hook.

Glancing up again, I realized what was in the air.

"Snow! I better get the heck out of here before it sticks to the ground!"

I was close to the car and hurried to it.

As a "seasonable tuber," I knew the time had come to reflect, read, and well, maybe fish for bass near home.

Tubing Big Reservoirs

It's easy to be negative when fly fishing and tubing a watery world which seems to spread out to infinity in every direction. I've wondered too many times just what in the heck I thought I was doing casting a fly in water big enough to hold a catfish that could swallow one of my legs. Nevertheless, these big reservoirs provide opportunities for fly fishermen and tubers that can't be overlooked. Lakes up to 1,000 acres are fairly manageable for anglers in a round "boat," but any body of water of 5,000 acres or more is huge for those who like tubing.

Big lakes generally hold more fish species than small ones thus giving fishermen alternatives for those days when trout refuse to strike. Such places are never boring. Even if the shoreline remains unaltered, there is always a new section to fish. Folsom Lake in the Sacramento Valley appears to be endless with the same rock or brush shorelines and, for that reason, it doesn't compel me to fish it on a regular basis, yet. When the lake is full, it would take a lifetime of fishing to cover all its coves and arms. Because I've seen trout to eight pounds come from ponds, I won't say that trout in sprawling reservoirs grow bigger, but since large stillwaters often have unlimited amounts of feed and cover, it is likely that big reservoirs might hold more big trout than small mountain lakes. Therefore, chances are probably higher for catching large trout on a consistent basis, particularly after the angler has learned an area well. Before fishing a great big place, it is a good idea to be sure the lake not only holds the fish species being sought, but also that it is one of the best lakes in the area for the kind of fish you want to catch. Almost all of the big valley lakes within 60 miles of Sacramento hold rainbow trout, but only a few have a solid reputation as a trout fishery. For best results, fish only the very best of them. If you haven't read the chapters on choosing lakes for bass or trout, please go over them before reading this one since much of what I say here buttresses what I already stated.

I'm about to fish Davis Lake, a 4,000-acre reservoir with 32 miles of shoreline. I have heard it referred to as the "best California mountain lake." For a state with literally thousands of trout lakes from sea level to 14,000 feet in altitude, that is quite a statement to make. Looking at a map of it, I see the west bank is a series of arms and coves and that the opposite bank is much straighter. Immediately, I know to fish the west side and around the islands out in the middle of the lake. Although I don't usually think of it, on a lake of this size it is a good strategy to tube a cove or two, cross to the opposite side, fish back to the car, and then drive to other likely areas. In fact, the car becomes invaluable to keep yourself on the shaded side throughout the day. Most of the time, I get too involved with the fishing (good, bad, or indifferent) to move around in this fashion, but, on big water, I think this approach makes sense. A quick survey while driving or wading often reveals what sections have the shade, cover, and structure. Frequently, a lake's contours tell much about what can't be seen under the water. For instance, grassy hills which gently slope into a lake usually create a wide shallow shelf. The bottom is likely to be mud or sand depending on the geographic area of the lake. In a woodsy or farm area, it probably is a mud bottom but on a high mountain plateau, the bottom is likely hard or covered with pebbles. If a stretch of shoreline is banked with the side of a cliff, I know such a shoreline quickly drops into deep water. When I do a survey, I search for logs, weeds, and brushpiles and I check for where a shallow ledge or shelf meets steep shorelines. Such observations are important whether I fish a small or large body of water.

On Davis Lake, I fished the west side since trees line it and provide shade, but, finding only shallow water without cover, I cross to the other side. Except for the mosquitoes, I was alone. It was the first time in years that I ever recall such a thick hatch of them. When they attack anglers, the underwater pupal stage has ended and is no longer a part of the trout's diet, therefore I fished with a brown Woolly Worm which is good from the first day of summer to the last day of fall. As I tubed along, I realized the many "coves' shown on the map were only slight indentations of the bank but an erratic shoreline usually attracts trout since it creates shallow and deep areas. Approaching a stump-filled indentation, I was ready for action as I thought of the big rainbows that swim in Davis Lake. Soon, I switch to a green Woolly Worm, but, even after retrieving it toward, away, and around the logs and stumps, nothing hit it. I kept kicking along as I gazed at the opposite side where I parked the car. The width of the lake expanded in the 100 yards I covered and, since the far grassy bank didn't intrigue me, I stayed on the west side. In mid-summer, I was surprised to be alone.

"Perhaps," I mused, "The boaters stay in the upper lake close to the dam and the island where the deep water attracts trollers."

I noted other interesting areas ahead of me and figured that eventually I'd find where the trout congregated, but, if it showed little promise of holding fish, it would be smarter to cross to the other side, fish back to the car, and drive until I found other likely spots to fish.

Switching to a yellow-brown hackle Woolly Worm, I stationed myself farther from the lake's side and fished deeper water. From the angle of the sinking line, I estimated that I had moved from eight-foot depths to 12 feet. Often, four feet makes all the difference in the world. Another way I estimate depth is with my thermometer stringer. In reasonably clear water, I look at the shiny thermometer dangling 3½ feet below the surface and, because of it, I estimate five to seven-foot depths by gauging how close it dangles to weed and rocky bottoms. I know a depth finder is the best way to be 100 percent accurate but, I recall a boating friend of mine telling me the deepest point of Becker Lake at normal water level is 28 feet. My estimation was 25 feet!

As I fished and swatted mosquitoes, hot sun rays almost cooked me alive. Although I carry repellent, I dislike using it because the odor sweats onto flies when I knot them to the tippet and I know fish dislike the smell. Preferring to have as much in my favor as possible, I not only kick softly in fishy areas but I also avoid anything that has an artificial odor. However, unable to take the bugs any longer, I set the rod under straps and put the creamy stuff on my face, neck, and hands. Near the bank, I rub my hands in mud hoping to mask the smell. Yet, I knew the effect might be 30 minutes at the most. It was one of the few days I wished for wind!

Soon, a fish hit the yellow Woolly. Thrashing its head back and forth, it surged for the middle of the lake.

"All right," I yelled.

I clamped my mouth shut when a mosquito almost flew inside it. The heavy vibrations throbbed through the graphite fibers and down to the cork grip. I enjoyed the first run and then pulled it toward me when the fish slowed down, but at the same moment, it changed direction and dashed away from me.

Pow! The popping of the 4X tippet seemed loud enough to be heard at both ends of 4,000-acre Davis Lake.

I gazed downward at the coils of line on the stripping apron thinking it must have been a three or four-pound trout. It may have been a bass, but, I think, the trout predominate. It had been a long time since I lost a fly to a fish (as opposed to snags). This fish made up for my lucky streak. After thinking about the trout and bass I've lost when I fly fish (almost 100 percent of the time) I concluded that I pulled the fly out of the corner of its mouth by playing the fish too hard. I went from one extreme to another. Finding the middle ground amounts to practice and persistence. There is nothing that can be written to truly convey how quickly or slowly to play a fish. I feel it is better to err on the heavy (fast) extreme since a lost fish definitely survives whereas there is the possibility a totally exhausted trout, particularly a rainbow, can die from a build-up of lactic acid in its system.

But, such knowledge did little for my spirit or ego that day long ago on Davis Lake. It turned out to be the only fish that struck during the nine hours I fished. Ever since then, I wondered if it might have been better fishing closer to the dam where the water might have been under 70.

This chapter represents some of my most recent reflections yet the idea of using the car to quickly get around accessible lakes and sectioning big reservoirs into smaller portions mentally or on a map is not only simple and effective but also one of the most obvious things to do. I feel like a dummy. Why didn't I think of it sooner?

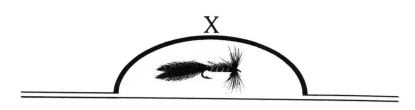

Deep Water Nymphing

To be successful fishing flies deep, four mental attitudes must be developed. Without them, the number of gadgets, flies, or fly lines stuffed in gear pockets are worthless. To fully understand a lake, its fish, insects, and forage fish, factors like weather, light intensity, changes in water temperature, water clarity, and daily or hourly movements of fish, bugs, and bait fish must be taken into account. It is a messy array of complications to consider. Keying in on these subtle changes is the most difficult thing in the world but it also is how to become a consistently successful lake fly fisherman. I think of myself as a student of trout fishing, not an expert. Too many times I have gone home skunked and bewildered. Yet I have also taken up to 30, two to four-pound trout a day. Most of my success I attribute to how I formed my fishing mental state of mind.

I am quiet and usually alone. One of the reasons tubing attracts me is that I don't create any unnatural sound in the water.

I doubt if I make more noise than a muskrat. To understand what is going on around you, you must be able to hear. Any extraneous noises like loud shouts, throwing rocks into the water, playing an instrument, (once, to my consternation, I heard a flute!), roaring boat motors, or radios blaring hide the natural sounds which when heard not only calm the inner being but also tune the mind to the slight changes of a lake's environment. There is nothing wrong with group fishing whether it's with several friends or families but to consistently catch trout of two pounds and over, the first thing to do is come to the lake with the proper frame of mind which is...being quiet!

I am observant. I look down, up, and around me as I sensitize myself to my surroundings. By heightening my senses, I can hear riffles kissing against a shoreline 40 feet away. If the day had been calm, a sudden riffle is a sign of a change which, believe it or not, affects an underwater organism — usually an insect or bug. Hearing the slight wind may be a sign to work a bit closer to the lake's edge and fish with a smaller fly. Noticing where shadows lengthen and decrease throughout the day indicate which side of the lake I should be fishing. Shorelines constantly change often in undramatic ways. Any curve, protrusion or cut bank is a potential "fishy" spot. Sticking my head toward the surface may look strange, but when I see underwater beetles diving up and down in the water or changes in the bottom contour, I just found clues for the day's fishing.

Sometimes, when tubing deep-water regions in the middle of a reservoir, a lake can surprise me. Too many times I'm caught off guard.

It happened to me one of the first times I fished Stumpy Meadows Lake in California. In the middle of its 320 acres, the lake could just as well have been 5,000 acres. I thought I could walk on its metallic smooth surface. My slow, even leg strokes almost put me to sleep. I rubbed my eyes which strained from the sun's glare, yawned, waved at two bait fishermen, and kept kicking, casting, and retrieving. I stretched my neck muscles straight back and to the sides. Stripping the fly toward me, it suddenly hung up on the bottom. Since the lake's bottom had been smooth, I peered into the water with surprise to see the bottom contours hump up toward me. My fly neatly lodged itself on a small rock as I crawled it up the incline. On the other side of the snag, I easily pulled the Zug Bug loose. Fishing the deeper water around the hump, I soon netted a few small rain-

HALF PRICE!
ONLY $9.98 FOR ONE YEAR

Flyfishing & Tying Journal (quarterly)

☐ **Yes**, send me *Flyfishing & Tying Journal* for one year for only $9.98.

☐ I prefer two years for only **$19.96.**

Name: _____

Card No.: _____

Please charge to my: ☐ Check Enclosed

☐ Check Enclosed

☐ VISA ☐ MASTERCARD

Expiration: _____/_____

Daytime Phone:(_____) _____-_____

Address: _____

City: _____

State: _____ Zip: _____-_____

0039

TOLL FREE 1-800-541-9498 • FAX (503) 653-2766
www.amatobooks.com

Frank Amato Publications, Inc. P.O. Box 82112, Portland, Oregon 97282

The author ready to tackle a lake.
Photo by Jim Primrose

All flies tied by Frank Flowers

All-Black Woolly-Bugger	**All-Brown Woolly-Bugger**
All-Brown Matuka	**Dark Spruce Streamer**
All-Black Matuka	**Muddler Minnow**
All-Brown Marabou	**All-Black Marabou**

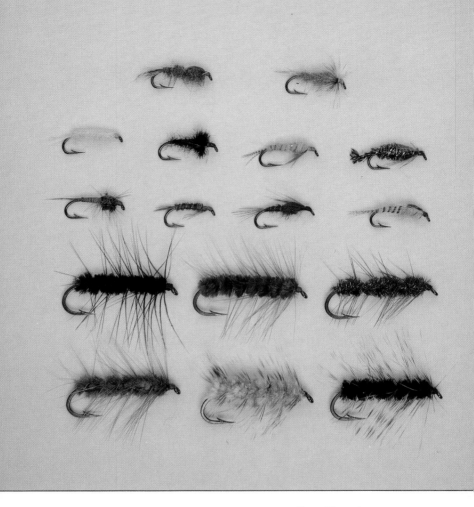

	Hare's Ear		Gray Nymph	
Cream Scud	Black Midge Pupa		Hare's Ear	Zug Bug
Dark Orvis A. P.	Pheasant Tail		Pale Evening Dun	Light Orvis A. P.
Black Woolly-Worm		Brown Woolly-Worm		Brown-Peacock Woolly-Worm
Dark Green-Brown Woolly-Worm		Gray-Grizzly Woolly-Worm		Black-Grizzly Woolly-Worm

Adams	American March Brown	Flying Fur Ant		Dark Cahill
Beaver	Black Gnat	Light Cahill		Leadwing Coachman
Brown Hackle	Brown Hackle Yellow	Wingless Ant		Gray Hackle Yellow
Dark Cahill	Black Midge	Brown Caddis	Gray Midge	Adams
	Dave Whitlock's Hopper	Light Cahill		Henry's Fork Hopper

Deer Hair

**Black
Hopper**

**White
Hopper**

**Red
Hopper**

**Yellow
Hopper**

Rod Robinson and Randall Kaufmann admire steelhead-size rainbow trout.

Very, very plump rainbow trout. Photo by Daren Erickson.

Plump rainbow trout.

bows. Until then, I had been fishless. Always be observant!

I am serious in intent. My goal is not just to fish or to catch lunkers, but to learn why and how things work. Fishing with this frame of mind changes everything. A fishless day is still worthwhile when some sort of understanding or knowledge comes through. It took forever to learn where the big trout in Arizona's Becker Lake were located. Since it is a high desert lake with few landmarks, I had to literally cover every inch of its 100 acres to sieve the good holding spots from the mediocre ones. Fishing from a tube made a big difference. In a boat, the temptation is strong to quickly cruise around from one place to another while dragging a fly off the back end of it. Holding the rod and moving slowly, I was forced to keep track of where the line and fly were in the water. Using book knowledge and correlating it to the particular stillwater I fished increased my ability to learn. It is one thing to read and know something but it is entirely different to take such knowledge and apply it. Most fly fishermen probably know nymphs and larvae grow thus providing the reason to have the same pattern in various sizes. But, do they know to what degree the bugs grow in a given lake?

In Becker Lake, small flies (numbers 14 through 18) are the best. The reason is that although *Callibaetis* mayfly nymphs rapidly grow and molt nine to sixteen times during their development, each new succeeding generation or brood is smaller. Trout must feed on them constantly. When I fished Becker Lake, I knew not only to use a smaller Hare's Ear nymph as the season progressed but also to progress from number 16 to number 12 nymphs in April and May prior to the *Callibaetis* nymph hatch when the nymphs matured and grew.

I do not disdain any type of fishing, whether it is catching small stocked rainbows on flies or sitting in a chair soaking up the sun as a bobber spins about in the wind. In fact, sometimes I need a break from serious fishing and drive to a put-and-take lake where I fling my flies about without too much thought and I catch freshly-stocked rainbow trout. Sometimes, when these lakes are crowded with lure, bait, and fly anglers, the stocked fish learn quickly and become a challenge to catch. It disturbs me when the serious angler is scoffed by anti-intellectuals and when smart people don't try to fish well or increase their knowledge of the sport.

I am persistent. Not much can be learned if an angler only fishes at dawn or dusk when he or she expects the fish to be feeding. It is understandable when a vacationing angler needs to maximize his time but a serious fly fishing float tuber owes it to him or herself to spend a full day on a lake. On a crowded fish-for-fun lake, most campers and local fishermen fish the first few hours of the day or at twilight but, to really understand the lake and to be able to consistently catch its eight-pound browns, it is necessary to study the lake all day long.

Sometimes I have a hard time understanding my fellow fly fishers. On one occasion (like many on my favorite trout lake), I tried nearly every pattern in all my fly boxes as I tried to figure out what the browns and rainbows were feeding on and I was almost fishless.

As the sun edged toward the rim of the earth, cars pulled into the parking area and boaters and tubers rigged up.

Soon, one of the tubers approached me.

"Hi," he said, "Are they hitting yet?"

"Been out since nine this morning. I got one about an hour ago."

He gave me a puzzled look.

"You've been out here all day?"

After re-casting toward the bank and resuming another slow strip, I responded.

"Of course!"

"It would bore me to fish here all day."

I gave him a puzzled look.

Fishing is never boring. Frustrating maybe. Long shorelines with miles of the same terrain is tedious to look at but the act of fishing is never boring. (My favorite lake is not big. It is small and scenic.)

I didn't say anything to him because I didn't know what to say. He went to the upper end and I stayed in the mid-section where I continued with my deep nymphing tactics. Persistence beats talent and genius any day of the week. Notice I wrote "persistence," not patience. To persist is actively pursuing and reaching a goal. To be patient is waiting for something to happen, like a fish chomping on a worm suspended in mid-lake with a bobber and split shot. Patience is not one of my virtues. Persistence is.

I am also prepared, as much as my limited funds allow. In an earlier chapter, I said two rods are better than one. In it, I told how to combine deep fishing with shallow fishing. A new idea hit me recently. Throughout much of the summer, especially in big deep lakes, I seldom picked up the second outfit because there isn't much surface activity. It might be better to spool the Wet Cel II Hi-D on the second outfit. I could easily fish down to 30 feet quickly. The Wet Cel II line is rigged with a 10-foot leader tapered to 4X while the Hi-D line has a five-foot leader with a 2X tippet knotted onto it. The combination allows me to switch tactics in seconds. One good summer combination is a crayfish pattern on the Hi-D line and a number 16 Hare's Ear nymph on the other one. Although seldom used, I have a wet tip line which I'm beginning to suspect is better for stream fishing. To be complete, I ought to take it off and replace it with a slow-sinking line. When I keep my casts short, my Wet Cel II does fine in the four to six-foot range, but I can probably do a better job with a Wet Cel I. Recently, I confirmed my suspicions by replacing my DT-7-F line with the Wet Cel I since I not ony snagged up less often but also netted trout otherwise uncaught. Brian Curtis, in *The Pursuit of Trout,* describes how he fishes from the surface to 25-foot depths with extra-long leaders, weighted flies, and floating lines. Al Kyte also describes the method in *Fly Fishing, Simple to Sophisticated.* My variation of it is to use leaders up to 12 feet and fish down to five-foot depths, but my recent experiments reveal that anchoring the fly on the bottom with a full-sinking line is better. Being prepared doesn't mean to stuff gear bags or vests with a huge array of flies. I have been impressed with many experts like Dave Whitlock, A.J. McClane, David Hughes, and John Gierach who advise a good rounded selection of flies which can be easily carried in less than four boxes. (There are many other experts. The four I mentioned represent the tip of the iceberg. Some day, maybe, I'll grab onto the underwater end of it.)

A stream thermometer and an old metal stringer with the loops removed is a primary tool for anyone who desires to be a "skillful tuber." A thermometer tells how deep to fish or how fast to retrieve a fly. Ninety percent of the time I inch my flies on the bottom, but when I note a sharp increase from 54 to 60 degrees, I bring the fly back in fast six-inch strips. Such a retrieve is undoubtedly better because insects are hatching and quickly ascending toward the surface. In fact, a quick change in the top layer of water also tells me I probably should use the floating line and a weighted nymph. Below 50, trout still feed and they can be conned into striking, but the fly must be fished slowly.

Seriously! There are more options to try when the water is too warm (above 70) since a warm trout lake holds more aquatic life than when it is 45 degrees. I have caught trout in water as warm as 73 degrees and as cold as 44. The thermometer is not to tell when not to fish but to indicate the amount of fish and insect activity to expect. At both extremes, the trout hug the deepest cover available or stay near springs or tributaries if they are available. When the incoming water is colder than the lake, sluggish trout of summer became active, but late in the year, colder incoming water repels them. A thermometer takes little room and is more important than adding a new fly box.

When I fish deep, **I become habitat oriented.** I want to be sure to fish all available types of cover. Each type of stillwater and its environs dictate what kind of cover is available to the trout. A desert lake may only have gravel and side contours while a forested foothill reservoir usually has cliffsides with sharp dropoffs and sunken timber. A valley lake seems to go on forever with miles of low-lying shrubs or trees all of which look the same. A farm pond or small natural lake usually has grass, weeds, and maybe a few stumps. The sides of an alpine lake often jut into a lake and create shoreline dropoffs while lower elevation reservoirs tend to have gradual-sloping lake sides. In a desert lake (the hardest to figure out), there are few signs for where a trout feeds or resides so it is necessary to cover all the water — the shoreline, edges, and middle of the lake, but don't just drag the fly and line around. Observe! When I began tubing Becker Lake (a high desert lake), I found, as I fished the center of its 100 acres, underwater hills of weeds which sometimes grew toward the surface. In any lake, weeds are where most insects are found. Consequently, trout are usually nearby. When I found those weed humps, I stopped and fished the dark holes in-between and soon caught a few rainbows. Being low in the water helps me see things most boaters speed by. Trout also like the edges where two sides of a desert lake meet. Slight curves and dents in the shoreline are also clues to depth changes. A forested foothill lake appears to be non-changing with its steep sides jutting toward the middle and miles of never-ending pine or oak trees, but make note that one point has reeds, another grass, stumps, or rocks. The very best areas are where two types of structure meet, like stumps and weeds. Fishing the almost bottomless middle stretches may seem to be a waste of time, but when I cross from one side to another, I keep the line out. Fish can't be caught with the fly on the stripping apron! Valley lakes, like around Sacramento, are usually frustrating. They hold endless acres of water and have miles of shoreline all of which look the same. They are likely to be the most common type of still water in the U.S. but because they usually have every kind of cover possible, their fishing potential is great. In my chapter on tubing big reservoirs, I give hints on how to break them down to a "tubing size." It takes great persistence to locate the right places but it's well worth it. Farm pond and mountain lakes are the most interesting to a tuber. When I fish one for the first time, I always fish the deep water beyond the shoreline breaks and circle the shoreline. But, I always look into the water and kick toward or away from the side in order to keep my fly in the deep water. A lake's shoreline sometimes is a long food shelf. Looking around me, I always search for different kinds of cover. True alpine lakes are characterized by bare rocks, tundra, and rocky shorelines without plant life. Without aquatic plants, they usually have little food life and therefore generally hold small trout, yet there are often small regions which are food-rich. To find them, it generally is best to stay close to the shoreline. The idea is to find gravel shelves between the steep dropoffs and rocky projections. I have yet to fish a true alpine lake above 10,000 feet but my experiences on Arizona's Knoll Lake or Woods Canyon, both of which rest near 8,000 feet, give me the alpine "feeling."

These different types of lakes — desert, forested, valley, mountain, farm pond, and alpine — hold different kinds of insects which dictate not only what pattern and size to tie on, but also what retrieve or method generally works best. Desert lakes, like Sunrise Lake in Arizona, hold surprises for the fly fishermen. Various mayfly, caddis fly, damsel fly nymphs, and midge larvae scuttle or bury themselves on or in the gravel bottom of such lakes. In Arizona, they are small (numbers 14 to 20). Throughout the year, a number 16 nymph proves to be the most effective. Nearly any fur pattern works. In the last chapter, I give a complete listing of fly patterns. A slow even strip is usually the best but as I use smaller flies I fish slower knowing the smaller organism generally move slower than bigger ones. Pausing, jerking on the line, changing the rod direction, and varying the speed of the retrieve are good variations to use. With a caddis imitation, I speed up the retrieve and make it jerkier, especially

with emerging pupa imitations. With a Woolly Worm, I use a
smooth three-inch strip followed by a pause. The brown Woolly
Worm or Hare's Ear nymph fished in this manner bring hard hits
from trout feeding on damsel fly naiads. Losing touch with the
bottom means the fly isn't deep enough. Weighted flies are less
effective, which is why I go to a faster sinking line. It's easy to be
hypnotized by a dull shoreline or a steady monotonous retrieve.
To stay alert, suddenly zip the fly into high gear, kick faster, turn
to face another direction, or form an "S" in the water. Once, on
Becker Lake, when I nearly fell asleep with my slow retrieve on a
fishless day, I formed an "S" toward a beaver dam. Just as I looped
around to make the bottom curve, my fly line straightened and a
fish struck. After a powerful run toward the middle of the lake,
the fish came my way, but, a moment later, it burst back into the
depths. We played tug-of-war for a few rounds before I finally
netted and released a 17-inch brown. My new strategy kept me
from being fishless.

Forested foothill reservoirs generally have less aquatic food
than desert stillwaters. Depending on altitude, dragonflies,
damselflies, or caddis flies predominate in such foothill lakes
but I have begun to suspect these reservoirs hold more forage
fish and "other foods" than insects. In these lakes of trees and
cliffsides, Woolly Worms down to size 8 seem more effective
than standard nymph dressings. The Wet Cel II Hi-D line is
generally more effective and, as opposed to the shallower desert
waters where shoreward casts usually produce the most fish,
parallel casts in lakes with steep banks do better. Apparently,
the trout rest on various ridges down the slopes and cruise along
the sides looking ahead for tidbits to eat. Surface feeding rarely
occurs yet the trout migrate up and down the sides therefore it
is a good idea to have the second rod rigged with another sinking line like a Wet Cel II. Regardless of lake type, when a hatch
finally occurs, it usually is intense but brief. Sometimes only 15
minutes. When my usual slow, even strip fails, I retrieve the fly
in jerks and pauses. The most effective technique anywhere is a
retrieve which mixes all types of line strips and speeds in one
long movement back toward the tube.

The mountain lakes, especially those with good weed
growth, provide the best array of insect life. Mayflies, caddis

flies, midges, and damselflies are all found in good quantities. Since the underwater forms of all these insect orders last several months and each order has several successive generations, deep nymphing is the best way to fish since there is always something happening. They might be out of sight but, rest assured, on the bottom, an array of insects, slither, or dart on and over the bottom cover. The Wet Cel II does all the work unless a lake's center is more than 25 feet deep. Because the major hatches occur near weeds or shoreline edges, casting toward the bank with nymphs and Woollies works the best. Slow and dead-slow strips catch not only the most but also the biggest trout. Mayflies and caddises are the most effective but, most of the time, I use number 16. The damsel naiads need a slightly larger fly — number 12 or maybe number 8. Midges vary in size but, most frequently, they need number 16 to number 20 imitations. One time, on Arizona's Rainbow Lake, I wondered what in the heck a big black bug in the surface film might be. I disregarded it and a few rising bluegill as I stayed on the bottom with my Wet Cel II line but, when I finally inspected the insect, I was amazed to see a midge which would require a number 10 dressing! Western anglers have good reason to carry a wide range of sizes when midging.

Most lakes I've fished over 8,000 feet in elevation I'd consider alpine in nature. Midges predominate in these reservoirs, yet I've had good success with Woolly Worms. Alpine stillwaters are among the prettiest places to fish and I enjoy their scenery, but when I go to one, I know not to expect many trout over two pounds. With my five-weight Far and Fine Orvis rod, I use my seven-weight Wet Cel II line. The combination allows me to fish deep and also have good sport with average-sized trout. The line zings out almost effortlessly even in a wind. The main thing to remember is to cast slow and smooth. The flies should be small. Some day, I intend to ask my fly tier if he'd make Woolly Worms on regular hook shanks. Tying them on number 12 or 14 hooks may be a chore, but I'm cerain such a tiny but "buggy" fly would be highly effective in any clear lake when the trout are highly skittish in the summer. Such a fly would become a standard dressing on high-altitude lakes since they are not only exceptionally clear throughout the year but also hold mainly tiny insects. Standard hackle wet fly dressings are exceptionally good in alpine waters. Casting a number 16 brown hackle (peacock) toward the bank and in the center of coves brings good action, but I still retrieve slowly and smoothly adding occasional pauses or jerks. It always seems odd to me to catch trout smack in the middle of a lake. Apparently, in alpine waters, trout often leave the shoreline more frequently than trout in lower altitude reservoirs. The lack of food and cover may cause them to cruise toward the depths with a higher rate of frequency than trout in other types of lakes.

There are many ways to retrieve a fly. I've zeroed in on the best method for a particular insect or type of lake. From books and my experience, here is a fairly complete listing of fly retrieves:

1) Three-inch strips in rapid succession
2) Altering between short and long pulls
3) Three long strips interspersed with long pauses
4) Dead drift while barely kicking
5) Short even strips
6) Barely inching it
7) Every strip varies in length with pauses between them
8) Each strip increases in length
9) Jerk the line, hesitate, let line drift off apron and start over
10) Hand twist
11) Lift fly off the bottom with rod and let it drift naturally back to the bottom
12) Fast "kick-troll" while quickly stripping the line

Don't forget the count down method which keeps the fly at the level where the fish are located. After casting count 1001, 1002, etc., until the fly hits the bottom. On successive casts, stop several numbers short of the last number to fish just above the bottom or cover where the trout usually rest. Often I crawl the fly on the bottom. It often snags but I also pick up my biggest trout down there. I find it amusing when an angler buys expensive rods and gear and then worries about losing a $2.00 fly.

In order to avoid the frustration of trying to find that "great fish hole" somewhere in the middle, pick several landmarks like a drop-off, outhouse, or mountain peak from two opposite directions. The point where the two right-angled lines intersect is the trout hole. By writing down the landmarks, they won't be forgotten. Find permanent things. A tree might fall. I've kept a logbook of all my fishing trips since 1970 and I put such information in it. Being faithful with such record-keeping is a large part of what it means to be a serious fisherman and a skillful tuber.

Bass Fishing

Now it's time to deal with farm and valley ponds and lakes. Here in the Sacramento Valley, the deeper, bigger reservoirs are stocked with rainbow trout which come toward the surface late in the year to feed on shad. They provide good sport throughout much of the winter, but this is specialized fishing.

I prefer to tell you about deep nymphing for bass. It's simpler than deep nymphing for trout, but simple doesn't mean easy. In fact, fishing in winter is usually slow, if not agonizingly slow. But between staying home and twiddling fingers or fishing, I'd like to doing the latter! I admit I don't tube as frequently in the winter as I do during the warm months since December through February are cold and wet but, between storms, the sun heats the air into the mid-50's and fishing is definitely possible. Since the water temperature is about the same as the air, I fish deep water off the points and long shelves with nymphs in sizes 8 and 6 or Woolly Worms in number 10 and 8. Just like smaller lures are usually better in cold water for bass so are smaller flies. I pick buggy patterns like the Hare's Ear and Gray nymph. The three best colors whether using a Woolly or nymph are black, gray, and brown.

The best bet is to follow the contours of the lake and fish in water at least 20 feet deep. Unless the lake is known exceptionally well, cast in all directions with the intent of covering all the water thoroughly. Often bass hang out in areas that seem barren on the surface. Kick slowly and barely twitch the fly. Try to imagine the hackles of a Woolly Worm undulating as it scuttles over a rock or log. Try to visualize the buggy fibers of a nymph puff as it creeps along the bottom. I know it's difficult to keep the mind and imagination energized but a keen imagination brings concentration. This increased degree of persistence is particularly needed when cold water slows down the bass's metabolism. When they hit, though, they kick into high gear and often fight their best. Maybe, it's their way to stay warm in cold water.

Here is a selection of retrieves to try on cold-weather bass when the water stays below 60:

1) Barely moving the line
2) Slow even pull of several inches
3) Pause and strip
4) Dead drift in the wind (with slight jerks)
5) Long strip, pause, inch the fly
6) No retrieve while slowly kicking or drifting in wind

Thus far, most of my experience is with largemouth bass. Smallmouth are likely to be more active in the winter. I know where to fish to find out! My "winter" bass fishing correlates to late October and November when in most other bass states the lakes freeze. The same tactics ought to work at that time. Even though I almost preach the slow retrieve-small fly routine, it is always good to experiment with other strategies but this method works about 75 percent of the time. A good analogy for new fly rodders is to think of jig or plastic worm fishing. The resemblance is amazingly similar. The nice thing about most bass nymphing is that there is minimal entomology to learn. Insects start hatching in warm-water lakes when the water begins to warm over 65 degrees. Now there are signs of bugs, damselflies, or dragonflies. An occasional mayfly surfaces but mides predominate in the shallow regions of a small lake. The damsel or dragonfly naiads are the main nymphs bass eat. Since they vary in color from brown to tan and green, it is good to observe how the immature forms look underwater. Out of the water, they are lighter in shade. The temptation is strong for many bass fly fishermen to use the biggest fly they can cast, but, when imitating an insect, it is definitely better to use the right size especially in hard-hit reservoirs. Often bass are as wary as any trout. As the water approaches 70, bugs and crustaceans become active. At that time, Zug Bugs and backswimmer patterns in number 6 and 8 do well. The very best retrieve is a strip and pause method combined with a 10-foot wet tip line. Although, in an earlier chapter, I recommended using two rods, I think many anglers get overly concerned with tackle and not involved enough with good old common sense and variations of fishing techniques. A long leader, weighted fly, and floating line duplicates the same action a wet-tip line gives a fly.

In early spring when the water is over 60, periodically fish in the shallows and deep water since the bass are now becoming active and migrating in and out of the depths. As it is appropriate, move shoreward and use the floating line and a weighted nymph or back off into the deep water regions and use a medium or fast sinking line. As the water warms to 70, quicker and snappier line pulls work better. Bass, on or near spawning beds, are aggressive and fast strips are effective on them. The trouble with spring is that it is brief. In fact, I've recently concluded that the "fast spring fishing" is earlier than most fishermen realize and is probably only a matter of weeks. Frequently, I took a good friend to my favorite bass lake not far from Sacramento and I'd tell him the bass were going to tear up our bass flies or popping bugs. We'd arrive at the lake after a 35-minute drive and I'd check the temperature. I'd tell him it was the "perfect" 72 degrees and we'd hook fish like crazy with flies and lures. I'd be in the tube and he'd be on the shore figuring that between the two of us we'd find the bass. But, toward the end of the day, we caught only a few small bluegill. Instead of fishing on a "perfect" day in mid-May, we probably should have been on the lake when the air first reached into the 70s and the water was in the high 60s. Even during the "prime" time whether it be March in a deep southern lake, April in a Sacramento Valley reservoir, or June in a northern state, the deep nymphing tactic is best except for when the bass are spawning in less than five feet of water. I can fish in shallow water by keeping my casts short. As the lake sides taper downward, I lengthen my cast until I finally try for the longest cast possible since such a cast converts into a long retrieve which is good for exploring all kinds of cover. As the water warms from 60 to 70, I strip the flies faster and with more jerks. In fact, anything goes, I think! But, after the bass leave the spawning beds and return to their cozy deepwater structures, I use the same strategies I described for winter fishing. The main difference is that in the summer there are more life forms available for the bass to eat. Often, bigger flies than I normally use are effective in the summer. Crayfish, leech patterns and Woolly Worms are excellent for summer use. The best Woolly Worm color is brown or black. In clear and/or hard fished waters, I stick with sizes smaller than six. I have yet to do well with crayfish imitations. Dave Whitlock's tactic is to use three or four-foot leaders which keep his fly right on the bottom. He jerks the fly along in fast strips and pauses. The technique certainly must work. He has a way of holding up huge bass for photographers, but he has been doing it longer than I have. The larger larvae and nymphs of burrowing mayflies are worth imitating, but throughout the bulk of the summer when I'm on a bass lake, I stick with the "buggy-looking" nymphs or Woolly Worms and I'm confident they will work.

In early summer, I cast shoreward but, as the days pass, I stay farther out searching for the sunken weedbeds or log piles where big bass congregate. My full-sinking line and sensitive graphite rod replace the expensive and bulky depth finder. The electronic gadget is much quicker but developing a fine sense of touch works and is reminiscent of the slow, easy-does-it style which seems to be missing in today's modern age of bass boats and array of meters measuring everything from sunrays to water temperature. A logical scientific approach combined with leisured fishing is not only productive but also the tonic needed for easing tensions.

Fall bass fishing is a mix of bass bugs, streamers, and fishing deep with nymphs. For me, it's late October through November. When I lived in Virginia and Missouri, it was September and early October. Since I prefer bass over two pounds, I stick with my sinking line and experiment with all retrieves. As the water cools to just below 60, the bass are moody one minute, liking a fly crawled on the bottom, and in the next minute chasing a fly stripped quickly. But, once the water stabilizes near 55, the bass settle near bottom cover usually not much more than 30 feet deep. At that time, they want a fly barely moving along.

When I lived in Missouri, Virginia, and Pennsylvania, I always hated the calm days in late November when brown leaves littered the ground and the water was approaching 40 because I knew by the end of the year the lake could be walked upon. I tried ice fishing less than a dozen times. If I didn't freeze my front or backside, I froze my fingers despite gloves since they had to be taken off periodically to handle the line or a lure. Besides bass seldom hit and any fish caught was quickly hauled up and thrown on the ice.

Now, I don't have to wait until April or May. Except for the days of heavy fog, rain, and cold spells, I can fish anytime, but I know that bass fishing in cold water is difficult. It is slow and tedious but the biggest bass are usually caught late in the year!

Two Approaches To Bucktail And Streamer Fishing

Bait fish are only one food bucktails and streamers imitate or suggest. In lakes from 8,000 feet down to sea level, tadpoles, leeches, worms, and large bugs crawl through the bottom cover and these food forms are not only eaten by trout but are also well-imitated with an appropriate bucktail or streamer. Often, large quantities of minnows or forage fish are slight in many trout lakes. Notice I specified trout. Most warm-water lakes have either large populations of minnows, bluegill, shad, or shiners. And for that reason, it's a good idea to imitate them. Most fly fishermen, I think, tie on a bucktail or streamer to either imitate a minnow or arouse a trout's attention. I suggest a third alternative — to imitate any large bottom creature which slinks, crawls, or swims near the bottom. Progressive fly anglers like Whitlock have made an art and science of this third aspect.

Most forage fish and bottom creatures prefer to stay in water no deeper than 20 feet and close to cover. A minnow can flutter a fin and hover near cover looking motionless, undulate its body as it swims around, or burst off like a rocket toward deep water when a big fish is after it, thus creating not only the first, most common, shallow-water approach but also the three main ways to work an artificial. Unfortunately, though, either the baitfish and/or the trout must be in the shallows in order for that technique to work. Usually the water needs to be over 60 degrees before the forage fish become active meaning that the best season of the year for this kind of fishing is summer. Since trout shun bright sunlight, the shaded side of a lake is more likely to be conducive for the typical streamer/bucktail type of fishing. The first hour of the morning is probably better for fishing near the banks than twilight judging by reports from fishermen but, as a night owl, I have a hard time trying to prove it!

When I first began fishing lakes for trout, I continually fished with marabou bucktails (the correct term for a Marabou leech) thinking either such flies were the best for lunker trout or that I could easily attract their attention with the "great" action I gave them. My intent was to appeal not to their hunger but to their curiosity or anger. I really don't care to document all the time spent fishing in this manner because it would be dull reading! Now, I'm dubious of this technique (for trout).

On one occasion when I fished with members of the Mesa Desert Fly Casters at Becker Lake, I was casting my bucktails from Al Williams' boat and he was outfishing me badly. With natural inclinations for persistence (which, when I'm not careful becomes stubbornness), I insisted I could catch trout on the marabou bucktails which I had had great success with when I fished Pennsylvania's Yellow Breeches Creek. I used almost every bucktail I had with vengeance as I watched Al Williams hook and net rainbow trout anywhere from 12 to 17 inches. After noting his line-stripping sequence, I pulled my fly the same way—still to no avail. The same thing happened when I fished with Frank Flowers who soon became my fishing buddy. Tired of inaction, I finally knotted on a Gray Nymph and within

10 minutes I boated my first trout of the day. With hindsight, I conclude: First, that the lack of a good minnow population in Becker Lake made the trout insect/scud feeders; Second, that trying to arouse a trout's curiosity is more difficult than appealing to their need to eat.

Over a year later when I began tubing and fishing deep, I changed periodically from one type of fly to another. I not only concentrated on being observant but also systematic. When I fished nymphs or Woolly Worms, my mind was geared for entomology but when I fished any sort of long-shanked fly, my thoughts were on bottom-hugging creatures most of which slinked from one type of cover to another. Tadpoles, leeches, and worms fall into this category. Although worms are seldom washed deeper than six feet, tadpoles and leeches roam as deep as 20 to 30 feet. At first, I thought the browns and rainbows which hit slow-moving Marabous were flukes until I compared how many I caught on the typical fast strip retrieve. Easily, the ratio was six to one. I don't intend to abandon the fast strip or shallow-water regions, but now I know that for consistent success for trout over 14 inches, one must fish a bucktail slow and deep. Such a fly imitates many things including forms of life which we may not be aware of. Fishing a brown Matuka or a Gary LaFontaine worm pattern right smack on the bottom and weaving it sideways with the rod tip may be reasonably accurate for an earthworms movements. Undulating a black Marabou bucktail in slow strips and changing the direction of the rod tip implies the behavior of a leech. Slightly faster strips with frequent pauses is suggestive of the erractic but slight movements of a tadpole. Some of my biggest rainbows hit Woolly Buggers (which I put in a streamer category) as I barely puffed them along. I can't be sure just what type of life such a strip suggests. I find it implausible the fish sucked up the fly out of curiosity or irritation. I've noticed strange-looking diving bugs in early-summer and I've wondered if they stay on the bottom throughout the remainder of the year. Perhaps the trout hit the Woolly Bugger thinking it was such a bug. Because I generally use modest-sized flies, I think that is fairly probable. It takes a lot of imagination, persistence, and thought to fish deep, but it is very worthwhile.

Deep fishing is not haphazardly casting from one direction to another. The most important thing to do is to orient all fishing in relation to the shoreline. It is important to note if the shoreline descends sharply or slowly into the lake. The second important factor is to note the available cover. Those are the best places for a resting fish. One prime area on a small lake I enjoy fishing in the Sierra Nevada mountains is a region of deep water which coincides with an imaginary line I draw between the two points jutting toward the middle. Any time I hook into a good fish, I make such imaginary lines because I want to fish the same water again. Sometimes it is close to shore where a line from a beaver dam crosses a patch of underwater weeds. When I'm in such a spot, I fish it hard and cover all the water by facing toward and away from the bank and also fancasting from left to right, but I always keep my fly on the bottom and I begin with the slowest of slow strips. When I'm satisfied I covered the whole area, then I experiment with other retrieves. As I do, I increase the speed and lengths of my line-pulls but only by degrees. I seldom change from a dead-slow strip to a super-fast one unless there is a particular reason. Usually, the best reason is when everyone is catching fish with that method!

Various retrieves I like for deep bucktailing are as follows:

1) Imperceptible tugs
2) Two-inch strips with pauses
3) A tiny jerk followed with an even 2 to 3-inch strip
4) Erratic tiny pulls
5) Hand-twist (least effective for me)
6) Twitch rod tip between pauses and even strips
7) Short tugs between natural drifts in waves
8) Short jerks against wave action
9) Long strips (6 to 10-inch) alternated with pauses or short pulls
10) Hand-twist combined with short strips

When I need to fish deeper than 25 feet, I use a Wet Cel Hi-D and a six-foot leader and stick with unweighted flies since they not only cast better but also have a more natural appearance and behavior in the water.

The sun rimming its way toward the horizon is a signal for trout fishermen to move shoreward and decide whether to dry fly fish or fish the shallows with nymphs or streamers. Over half the time, I tube toward the side of the lake and concentrate on the deep water regions just under the food shelves, but I'm always looking for rises or fish splashing in the shallows. Sometimes, mainly to change the pace or to keep from being too loyal (stubborn?) with my deep fishing tactics, I switch to the rod with the floating line and fish close to the bank. I seldom dry fly fish. Often, while small to average-sized trout feed on rising insects, big trout feed underneath them either on nymphs or minnows. A fair compromise is to pick up the rod with the floating line rigged with a 10 to 12-foot leader which allows a fly to sink to the mid-depths (four to six feet) yet it still is easy to fish in shallower water or on top.

My first shallow water technique is to kick parallel with the lake's contours and cast shoreward. In order not to scare fish, I keep some deep water between myself and the shoreline. Some writers advise picking up the line when deep water is reached, but too many times as my fly sinks deeper just prior to my roll cast, a fish strikes. It's possible a trout followed the fly and went for it just as the bucktail disappeared toward the depths. Now I purposefully let the fly sink and continue with my retrieve or give the fly a sudden twitch. Such a tactic brings the kind of strike which jolts a sleepy tuber awake. When I see a rock pile or a loggy shoreline, I stop, face it, and fancast the area with a large array of retrieves. With the floating line, stop and go retrieves are particularly effective since the streamer sinks and rises in the water as if it were an injured minnow. Usually, fishing minnow-like flies shallow means faster and more erratic strips. The following retrieves usually work:

1) Four-inch quick pulls
2) Four-inch strip followed by a slight tug
3) Two-inch strips interspersed with pauses
4) Slow, even six-inch strips and a hesitation
5) Let the fly sink to the bottom, pause, then jerk it
6) Haul it in as fast as you can
7) Do like above but pause between the pulls
8) Grease the fly and tug it up and down in the surface

To tell you the truth, although I've often read about it, I've never done number 8. The idea just doesn't appeal to me, but I'm sure it works for all kinds of fish. I remember reading about a floating minnow pattern constructed out of balsa wood, but I never did buy one. Nobody seems to advertise it anymore, but, it worked like a Rapala and ought to be great as daylight surrenders to darkness or as the first weak rays of sunlight illuminate the earth.

If you recall, in an earlier chapter, I described the two-rod system. If I knew a lake had exceptionally good populations of minnows and baitfish, I'd have a black Marabou bucktail on my sinking line and a close imitation of the predominant forage fish on the other line.

Many anglers use big patterns with the intent of catching a muskie-sized trout, but, in most places numbers 10 through 4 bring consistent hits from trout up to two feet long. In crowded waters, smaller flies do better for me. I use number 8 the most. It's big enough to catch big trout and also hooks well in a fish's mouth. Wider gaps not only take more force to hook a fish well but are also more easily shaken from a jumping trout's lip. I admire those who wait for that one huge trout which is invariably caught at night when I prefer to do other things. The best "lunker hunters" don't just persist and hope for the best. They fish at night, in nasty weather, at dawn, and early and late in the year. They intimately learn only one lake with a reputation for big trout and study the habits of not only the fish but also the food which the big trout eat. They are also obsessed.

As a daytime fisherman, when I do things right (I don't always!), I expect to land trout up to at least 20 inches. They are plenty of sport on my seven-weight Orvis All-Rounder! Always talking with fishermen, I enjoy learning how other men and women fish and why. If we all had the same goals, we fishermen would be a dreary bunch, wouldn't we?

In fact, it's now time to come down into the valley and lowlands to check on the methods of the bass bucktail fly fisherman.

Bass Fishing

I'm a rebel when it comes to bass streamer fishing — I don't use the great big sizes usually recommended for bass. For one thing, they don't cast well on a seven-weight fly rod and I'm not about to buy a nine-weight outfit simply to cast huge bucktails. One of these days I'd like to have the Orvis nine-by-nine, but most likely it would be used for salmon, steelhead, and striped bass. Second, in most warm water lakes, shallow water bass are easily frightened by unnatural noises. Big flies splat heavily in the water; small ones don't. Third, a bass is more likely to suck in a small fly (or lure) and only lip a large one. Therefore, hook penetration is better with the small fly which is also less easily shaken by a bass thrashing its head back and forth in the air. Fourth, the most common size of baitfish most bass eat is from two to three inches. I was surprised to learn this fact both from Homer Circle's and A.J. McClane's writings. Most number 4, three-by-one bucktails are over three inches long. Fifth, because of the thinness of a small (sharp) hook point, smaller hooks take less effort to hook a fish. And sixth, with smaller patterns, I never know what might hit since large bluegill, crappie, and even catfish strike them. Yet, at the same time, a big bass might strike it. Once, on a foothill California bass lake, I hooked a six-pound largemouth on a number 8 black Marabou bucktail. To purposefully fish for the big ones, use number 2 and larger patterns, but fish only at night, during the first hour of the day, on bad weather days, and late in the year.

Tubing at night is risky and I don't recommend it. Just when I thought I knew a small lake well enough to fish and tube after the sun set, I discovered an underwater stump during a low-water period. In fact, I almost kicked into it and I swiveled away just in time to miss having a sore ankle. Constantly, while I tube, I turn my head around in order to see where I'm going. Is a 10-pound bass (or trout) worth a cracked ankle bone? Tubing is a daytime activity.

Most of the time I tie on number 8 or 6 streamer flies to 4 or 2X tippets. The light leader not only helps deceive wary fish in clear water (which I find frequently) but also gives the flies better action. A number 6 bucktail on a 4X tippet sounds like heresay, doesn't it? But, I've been fishing that way for most of my adult life! I seldom lose fish due to hard strikes (from me or the fish). Sometimes a log or rock steals a fly from me, but well, who said life was perfect? If I don't regularly feel the bottom and its cover, my fly isn't deep enough. In comparison to having an expensive graphite rod broken or stolen, losing a $2.00 fly is not a great problem—unless I lose a dozen or more during a day's fishing, but I don't. A great advantage of tubing is the relative ease of unsnagging flies from the bottom. I only recently realized that my inclination not to fish from a shoreline is that I'd miss the things I can do when I'm in the tube.

Bass tend to stay closer to the sides of a lake than trout throughout the warmer months. I find this to be true both when I observed them living together in peaceful co-existence in the same lake or when I compared my results fishing a mountain trout lake and a lowland bass reservoir. This doesn't mean that bass don't wander into the depths, but only that, as a cold-water fish, trout seek the coolest temperatures found in the deepest portions of a lake. The word "deep" is relative. In a 50-acre body of water, deep may be 15 feet whereas, in a big reservoir, deep is likely to be 40 feet. The foregoing must sound 100 percent wrong compared to what the professional tournament bass fishermen write, but remember, I'm a bass fishing rebel! Nine out of ten professional bass pros seldom fly fish or tube since they constantly seek the "holes" where the lunkers rest. I don't blame them. How else can they win tournaments? Bass of 10 pounds and over have different habits from the "runts" and mid-sized ones. My "in-between" bass generally stay in the intermediate depths (10 to 25 feet) which are most frequently the deeper extensions of the shoreline contours after the first edge breaks into mid-lake regions. Usually, I'm within 60 feet of the lake's edge. When I fish lakes which also hold trout, as summer progresses, trout head for the river channel on the bottom, near inlets, or springs, but the bass suspend themselves about halfway down the shoreline slopes.

The best strategy, therefore, is to face the side of the lake and kick away from it until the right depth is found. In fact, an excellent system is to bass bug or fish streamers in the shallows at dawn and, as each hour passes, fin out about 10 feet and fish deeper. When the fly can't be felt on the bottom, it's time to use the sinking line.

I love the slurp of a bass smacking a surface lure and its aerial stunts but I also love to catch them on a regular basis, therefore I use underwater flies most of the time, even as the skies darken. Although I can't prove it, I have a theory that the harder a bass lake is fished the less frequently bass over two pounds migrate to the shallows for their morning or evening meal. I recall too many times when Ken Townsend or Bill Crofford and I pried our eyes open at 4:30 a.m. in order to fish Virginia's Burke Lake or Occaquan Reservoir just before the sun spread a soft glow across the sky. But, instead of catching the fish of our dreams, we seldom caught more than one or two yearling bass. Disappointment quickly set in and we almost nodded back into dreamland as we hoped for a bass to attack our bass bugs. They are two of the hardest-fished lakes in Northern Virginia. In retrospect, I now realize we did better at Lunga

Reservoir because it was on the Quantico Marine base which was restricted to military families. I guess it was good my dad spent most of his life in the Army! If I desired bass over two pounds on a consistent basis I learned that I had to fish the bottom. Spring, of course, is the main exception, but even then, as Jason Lucas, *Sports Afield's* previous fishing editor reported, the best bass feed below the smaller ones. It all depends on what you want.

When beams of the sun reflect strongly off a lake's surface, it's time to be at least 10 feet deep or more. Still facing the shoreline, I kick toward mid-lake. When the bass are found, fishing parallel is good since the fly not only stays at the right depth but it can then be discovered how far the bass roam along a given stretch of shoreline. As the sun grows brighter and reaches toward its zenith, bass migrate into deeper water so I kick farther toward mid-lake but I still usually find that shoreward casts work the best. Late in the afternoon, bass migrate closer toward the sides of a lake as the sun moves toward the horizon. I turn to face the center of the lake and tube with the movements of the fish. In the last hours, just before daylight surrenders to the night sky, unless there are constant rises and splashes, I stay on the bottom. Sometimes I'm greatly pleased with what I find.

I followed my own advice (for a change) when I fished Amador Lake, a private lake and resort where the owners charge a fee for fishing and boating. Toward the end of the day, I barely managed to knot a number 8 black Marabou bucktail in the last few minutes of twilight. I didn't begin my retrieve until I felt the fly scratch bottom. Halfway back toward me, a fish struck and skyrocketed toward the surface creating a wide loop in the sinking line. It happened the instant I struck. Then the bass leaped into the air, sprayed half the lake into the air, and dove back toward the bottom, but when it did, it tugged against the tension of the line. The belly of the sinking line tightened and popped the fly from its mouth. I didn't have time to breathe let alone raise the rod hoping to eliminate the nasty belly of the line.

I was fishing Amador Lake because I knew it had Florida-strain largemouth bass. I've caught plenty of bass up to three pounds. The one which stole my bucktail was at least twice that size. I still shake thinking about it. Although I lost it, I wouldn't have had the thrill of hooking it if I had changed to the floating line and a bass bug.

The approach of moving from shallow to deep and back to shallow is most effective when the angler knows exact areas where the bass hang out. On a new lake, it's better to tube parallel with the lake's contours. With each new circle around a small lake or any given cove, I kick 10 feet closer toward the middle as I search for fish and underwater cover. Even if bass aren't found, it is a good idea to triangulate an area where deep weed beds and log piles are found since those are prime places for the biggest bass in any kind of lake and, sometimes, such areas are out in the middle. After a number of "fishy" shoreline stretches are located, the shallow-deep-shallow routine can be used.

Normally, I fish bucktails and streamers in moderate strips, but I have a repertoire of retrieves I rely on throughout the day. These are among my best:

1) Short strip, pause, long strip
2) Long even strips without pausing
3) Long even strip, pause, short strip
4) Bring the fly back as fast as possible
5) Dead drift in wind between short pulls
6) Quick short strips and "kick troll" at top speed
7) Long quick pull and let fly settle back to bottom
8) Let fly rest on bottom – then dart it to life
9) Jerk rod tip to the sides between strips
10) Form a figure-8 toward the side of lake

Marabou and Woolly Bugger type streamers work the best for me, but Matukas and Muddler Minnows are also excellent patterns. Standard bucktails like the Black Nosed Dace or Mickey Finn are less effective in stillwaters than conventional streamers like the dark or light Spruce, but neither type compares to the Marabous or Woolly Buggers. I don't like the term "Marabou leech" because the pattern can imitate many forms of life depending on how it is moved in the water. Should I refer to a Muddler Minnow as a nymph because it also looks like many bottom foods as well as sculpins?

Marabou bucktails can be tied in at least two styles. The one I prefer is with all of the feather on top of the shank because it gives a clear streamlined appearance in the water and works much better than the bushier type in clear and hard-fished lakes. But I also carry the other type which has the Marabou feather tied above and below the hook shank. It is supposed to be better as skies darken and in stained waters but I have yet to prove it to myself. Because they are bulkier, they don't cast easily especially in a wind, but I think they're worth having.

Weighted flies are not only hard to cast but also are less effective for me. I believe streamlined, fairly sparse, and moderate size long-shanked flies are much more imitative of baitfish and other trout foods and, on a sinking line and short leader, they sink naturally toward the bottom. Rather than adding weight to help a fly along, I switch to faster sinking line and a shorter leader.

Regardless of how you approach the lake and of your retrieve, stick to smaller sizes like number 6 or 8. Just maybe, like me, you'll become a "bass rebel!"

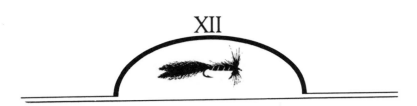

XII

Wet Fly Fishing For Rising Trout

Although I have a box of dry flies, I rarely use them when I fish a trout lake even when the trout are rising. It may be a damselfly, midge, caddis or mayfly — the "big four" for trout lakes — I still don't fish a dry fly. Maybe I'm spoiled. When I fished streams in Pennsylvania, a hatch really meant something. A dense cloud of insects hovered near the surface of the stream and all of the trout from tiny ones to big ones stationed themselves and continually rose to the insects drifting toward them. Still, to this day, I can visualize the White Mayfly (Leucron Mayfly spinner) flying down from the trees half an hour after darkness set. The cloud of insects was almost thick enough to be mistaken as a cloud in the sky. The mayfly spinner created beautiful mayhem on the trout of Yellow Breeches Creek, but I didn't need the mayhem of fly fishermen who suddenly became grabby, greedy, and sometimes belligerent.

In the trout lakes of Arizona and the Sierra Nevada mountains east of Sacramento, although many provide excellent fishing, clouds of any sort of insect don't exist. After a decade of tubing after trout, I remember maybe a dozen intense hatches which brought up large trout. Half were damselflies and the rest were midges. In fact, the black midge hatch was the first one I witnessed on a lake. On one California lake east of Redding, I fished during a strong mosquito hatch but it only brought up the small trout. I remember it because I had been fishless and suddenly trout slapped the surface sometimes within grabbing distance of the tube. The excited trout made splashy rises which had me thinking of a caddis hatch, but leaning toward the surface, I soon realized that wasn't the case. The difference in a mosquito and a midge isn't readily observable until the insect is scrutinized. Only 15 minutes passed as I made these observations and tied on the right fly, but, in that time, the hatch was already winding down. Brief and intense are the best descriptions of most trout lake hatches. With the exception of the damsel fly, hatches seldom last longer than half an hour. It takes not only perfect timing but also an accurate prediction to do well dry fly fishing lakes. Unlike streams, the insects of stillwaters are too unpredictable to be able to figure out a hatch timetable.

When the good trout are roused by insect activity, they cruise and pursue the insects creating a "cruise lane." Remember, in a lake there is no current to send a fly to a trout and they have to expend energy to eat a rising fly. The need to go after them prevents the larger trout from leaving the bottom until there are either enough insects or big nymphs or duns to worry about. Midges nearly always hatch in clouds and damsel fly naiads are sizeable. Therefore, trout over 14 inches come up for them. Yet, I still don't use a dry fly. In a damsel fly hatch, the naiad is the center of concentration and it swims like a tadpole just under the surface. In a midge hatch, the focus is on the pupa. It took me forever to discover the facts of midge feeding trout and I wish I had a dime for every fishless cast I made to a pupa feeding trout. I'd be the richest man in the world!

These, of course, are only general rules and trout love to break them. I know there are times when a dry fly is appropriate but thus far, most of the surface feeding trout I've caught were victims of my wet fly methods.

With slight variations, I use wet patterns during the precious moments when a caddis bursts skyward, a mayfly dun floats on the surface, or a midge tries to escape from a trout. On lakes, most caddis flies I've met were small. With the feathers of a number 16 Dark Cahill slanted low to the shank, I have a wet fly highly suggestive of most caddis pupae found on lakes. A wet Adams, Leadwing Coachman, or Pale Evening Dun tied in a similar fashion represent the main other colors for lake caddis flies. Instead of waiting to figure out which way a cruising trout went, I cast right to the rise. When I manage to lightly drop the fly just to my side of it, the presentation is perfect. Since the trout are always moving, the cast must be quick and accurate. Immediately upon descent, I erratically and quickly strip the fly toward me. When the timing is right, the trout hit as soon as I begin my retrieve. If it doesn't, I assume the fish hurried to my right or left but, no matter, I continue bringing the fly toward me until it's within three or four feet of the tube. Often, another feeding trout in another "cruise" lane sees my fly sinking and rising near the surface and it hits my wet fly with a jolt that tremors down the rod and to my hand. This tactic has worked on caddis-feeding trout on Arizona and California lakes and it should work in other regions of the U.S. I estimate it works 60 to 70 percent of the time. During the other 40 to 30 percent, I scratch my head and ponder as I experiment with other methods like skittering a dry fly. In fact, it took a number of skittered bedraggled dry flies which caught trout and had me thinking of wet patterns for rising trout. Although brown number 16 flies predominate, to be complete, a range of sizes from 14 to 22 is good to have.

The retrieve is different when a mayfly surfaces. In lakes, the most common species is the *Callibaetis* which is a strong swimmer. Longer quick strips seem better. With this hatch, a slim lightly-hackled Hare's Ear nymph is the most effective. There are also exact *Callibaetis* nymph imitations available and in a super-clear lake where trout are highly selective and wary those patterns might be necessary. Other wet patterns like the Light Cahill, Pale Morning Dun, Hare's Ear, and March Brown are good imitations of other mayflies I've encountered.

I'm still observing and experimenting with the midge flies, but thus far, I know a steady and deliberate retrieve is best and that accuracy is important when these tiny creatures are hatching. In a strong midge hatch, the trout do less cruising and tend to station themselves at a certain location. Midges can be of almost any hue, but where I fish, black, gray, and yellow predominate meaning pupas or a wet hackle fly in those shades do best but the flies must be small — number 18 to 22. Yet, sometimes, a large midge species confuses me. Out West, in some regions, it takes a number 10 midge pattern to match the insect. Black and gray species are universal and are found almost anywhere.

Wet hackle patterns like the brown hackle-peacock or gray-hackle-yellow body are among the oldest known to fly fishermen and they even go back to the days of Izaak Walton. Yet, they are one of the most underrated types of wet flies today. Our fancy nymphs often with molded parts and distinctive segments look great, but I have yet to find any of them consistent fish takers. I'll take a basic assortment of fur nymphs and wet hackle patterns any day of the week. In fact, my favorite summertime pattern is a number 16 wet brown hackle-peacock body. I crawl it on the bottom and fish it in the film. Although they are tailor-made for midge pupa-feeding trout, I find hackle wet flies are an excellent all-purpose fly from the first day of the season to the last day in November. I cannot count the number of times when my fellow fishers from fly rodders to bait anglers went fishless and approached me asking how I just caught an 18-inch rainbow. Skeptically, they looked at my tiny fly on my 4 or 5X tippet and I knew they probably wouldn't give such a fly a decent workout. I don't attribute my success to any great "expertise" but to the willingness to learn and experiment...until I find that method or fly that consistently works. And the wet hackle flies and dead-slow retrieve is such a strategy.

Most of the time, midges hatch close to the shoreline. Stationing myself just beyond the edge, I cast shoreward specifically to a rising trout. It does little good to cast a midge imitation haphazardly hoping for the best. If the intended fish doesn't strike, I let the fly remain motionless as I look around for another riser. I don't like the mess of fly and leader floatants, but I realize that is the standard way to fish a midge pupa. After a long pause, I bring the fly toward me with a slow, even strip usually less than an inch in length. I continue looking for another riser. Frequently, the movements of the fly bring a strike, but if a fish doesn't hit, I either re-cast toward another trout or continue bringing the fly toward me. When I reach the edge, I re-cast back into the shallows. Sometimes I let the fly sink to the bottom as I wonder if any more trout are about to rise. Quickly pulling the fly off the bottom sometimes brings a ferocious strike. I recall only one time on a small lake off Bowman Lake Road, in the Sierra Nevada Mountains, when a light midge hatch came off in the middle of the lake and my small wet hackle fly caught small rainbows on almost every cast.

There has been much said about two, three, and four-weight fly rods particularly as a tool for midging but I believe a slow full-flexed action rod up to seven-weight does fine. A five-weight outfit is ideal since it is powerful enough to handle light wind and yet is sporty and will cushion light tippets. Although I've used a six-foot wand while float tubing, eight-foot is much better. When choosing fly rods for tubing, it is wise not only to consider the weather but also what hatches to expect on a given day. One time, on my favorite Sierra Nevada trout lake, I rigged up my two seven-weight rods since the day was windy. Later in the afternoon, as soon as the wind died, a midge hatch surfaced. Although the car was nearby, I couldn't trust the hatch to be long enough to rig up my five-weight rod. The floating line was rigged on my crisp Cortland graphite rod since I like to use my Orvis All-rounder with my Wet Cel II line. I cast a black midge pupa to a riser and it took the fly. I barely tugged on the line in response to the strike but, in the next instant, the trout tore free of the fly and I swore. It should have been my first trout of the day. The stiffness and taper of the medium-action rod worked against me. I grimaced thinking that I knew better than to use such a rod when midge fishing. I had two outfits on the tube and I switched spools with the Orvis Full-flexed All-Rounder. The slower action and slimmer taper cushioned both the fish's and my strike. With the exception of when I poorly played a fish, I seldom lost them. When I rig up at the car, I now try to predict what type of insects might hatch.

I'd estimate that my wet fly techniques on rising trout work over half the time. When they don't work, even standard dry flies fail, but I keep persisting, observing, casting, and changing flies always trying to raise the score. But batting 600 isn't bad!

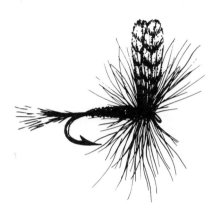

XIII

The "Other" Trout Foods

It's summer and the metallic sheen of your favorite trout lake makes you think you can walk on top of it. The 72-degree water makes you think of bass and bluegill. You shrug and slouch your way back to the car trying to think of what else to do besides fish. If you're like me, during those long summer days, there really isn't much else you want to do but fish. So what if the lake looks impossible? Fish anyway. It's what makes you feel good, right? And, if you're careful, you might even catch a few trout. Even if they are only 10 to 14-inchers, isn't a day of tubing better than paying the bills or mowing the lawn?

There are "other" trout foods besides the insects which are now long gone, and they can save the day. Every lake and every geographic region is different, but, for me, snails have been the most important. Imitating snails has little romantic appeal but trout love snacking on them. Any crustacean-eating trout quickly grows and puts on weight since these foods are rich in protein. It is a lucky angler to be near lakes supporting scuds, crayfish, and/or snails.

One time in the middle of summer as I tubed my favorite lake in Arizona, I wondered what was floating on the surface until I approached it and discovered empty snail shells. On occasion, when the oxygen level of the water is low or when cloudy skies blot out the sun rays, snails rise from the lake's bottom and begin a mass migration. I have yet to see the slow march of the gastropods but the presence of their shells must mean something. I commenced to find an appropriate fly and present it to the bottom-feeding trout. It took plenty of perseverance and imagination but eventually I found a reasonable solution.

A thickly-tied chenille fly with a fluff of a hackle at the head not only looked ridiculous but it didn't work. Scud patterns also failed but I admit my lack of confidence in them prevented me from giving such flies a thorough testing. Then, I tried various nymph patterns until I had a strike. It was about time!

Soon, I brought in a thick-muscled rainbow over two pounds and it was stuffed with snail shells. Now, I had to be sure it wasn't a fluke. I cast, let the line and fly settle on the bottom, rested it there for a while, and quarter-inched the fly along the bottom and back toward me. I yawned and my head nodded, but a moment later, I felt resistance. I struck and played another heavy fish. After the sixth trout, I was convinced the ultra-slow retrieve parallel with the bank in 20-foot depths and with a number 12 American March Brown Nymph was the answer. Successive trips throughout the summer verified my findings and I reported it to my fly tier, Frank Flowers. Sometimes, in blustery weather, the snail-feeding trout went almost crazy and I took up to 30 trout over 14 inches in a day's fishing. Why, didn't I have my 35mm Canon Sprint back then? Especially when I netted and release an 18-inch rainbow which weighed almost four pounds.

The next most important trout food in summer is the leech. Some anglers would probably argue that the crayfish is the number one or two "other" trout food. If I were to rate these summertime trout foods by quantity, I'd agree with them but, for catching trout, I disagree. Maybe, the number of mini-lobsters in some of the White Mountain lakes in Arizona is like a heavy hatch of mayfly spinners – the artificial is lost in a sea of insects moving and fluttering in ways impossible for even the best anglers to duplicate. I wonder if the crayfish imitations are too exact and not "buggy" enough. I've fished with the available patterns on the recommended fast sinking line and ultra-short leader when the water warmed over 60 which is when they become active, but despite my erratic retrieves near rocks, I have yet to catch a trout on such a fly.

But leeches and leech imitations are another story! They live on land as well as on a lake's bottom. Like snails, they like mud bottoms, logs, and vegetation and an abundance of bottom debris mixed with dead organisms. Leeches swim with bodies elongated and move in wave-like motions traveling a foot in about three seconds. They also stay near the bottom. They migrate as deep as 25 feet. Often, they move about during low light periods or when the wind whips up.

Since they are predominantly dark in color, brown, gray, or black Woolly Buggers or Marabou Streamers imitate them well. Dave Whitlock and other famous tiers have highly realistic leech patterns like the Chamois leech but I've done fine so far with the more suggestive patterns. I prefer them since such flies resemble a wide array of insects, bugs, and "other" trout foods.

I've been surprised fishing small (numbers 8 and 6) Woolly Buggers and Marabou flies in the middle of a lake and getting hits where I least expect a trout to be as I crossed from one side to another. I don't bring in the fly simply because I quickly tube from one hole to another. It's fun being waylaid by an unexpected trout! In fact, now, I often purposefully tie on a leech pattern just before I leave a spot especially if my destination is a considerable distance from where I've been fishing. When I think of leeches, I fish the "bugger" and marabou bucktail with slow even strips of maybe two to four inches but, when I want to wake up the fish, I strip the fly back quickly as if it were a minnow streaking away from a hungry trout.

The rest of the warm-water trout foods are fairly equal in my rating system because scuds, waterboatmen, backswimmers, sowbugs, tadpoles, eels, and salamanders are seldom found in high concentrations, except for maybe scuds. I group tadpoles, eels, salamanders, and leeches in one group because they not only like the same kind of bottom cover but are all imitated with the same kind of flies and methods. Remember, it is more important to know when, where, and how to use a fly rather than overloading tube or vest pockets with different patterns.

Keep in mind that most bottom feeding trout quickly switch from one type of food to another throughout a 12-hour day. The way they feed is similar to people in a cafeteria line taking what looks good to them. But, trout also have a way of breaking general rules. When good observations on a given lake indicate trout resting in unusual places or concentrating on a particular kind of food, disregard book knowledge and apply common sense. The idea is to catch them! Not to rigorously follow an "experts" advice or rules.

Backswimmers and waterboatman are diving beetles of the order *Hemiptera* not a woman swimming on her back or a good-looking hunk in a boat! Both beetles have nearly identical habits. They are active for only brief periods in spring and fall. It takes a good observer to see one. Being in a tube and close to the waterline helps. Once, I recall watching a waterboatman at Becker Lake and I blinked at the beetle diving up and down in the water. But, it was only one. I continued fishing my Woolly Worm on the bottom. The beetle looks somewhat like a flattened football or maybe a small boat. They hatch from an egg, have five nymphal molts, and a winged adult stage. They are seldom over half an inch in length. I think small weighted nymphs on a floating line and a 10-foot leader or a wet-tip line would work, but if there were a "hatch" of them, exact imitations might do better, expecially in a fish-for-fun lake. Dirty-yellow, brown, and gray are common colors. A Hare's Ear Nymph or a Gray Nymph ought to do it.

Unlike most insects, the beetles shun weed-beds preferring semi-barren areas. The sink and strip method on a floating line not only relieves the tedium of slow deep fishing but may also attract the attention of a semi-dormant trout. I hope I remember this idea the next time I'm fishing.

Most fishermen call a scud a freshwater shrimp probably because that is what it looks like. They belong to the order *Amphipoda* of the class Crustacea, therefore they are close relatives of the crayfish. Just maybe, the best advice for catching big rainbows or browns on flies is to concentrate on lakes (or streams) which have a large population of scuds. Trout love them and they grow fast on this protein-rich food. Trout can gain from a pound to two pounds a season in a scud-filled reservoir. The little crustacean lives in bottom cover like decomposed leaves, moss, or debris and usually stays in the shallows. They become scarce as the shallows curve toward the depths. They inhabit alpine lakes of 12,000 feet and lakes down to almost 4,000 feet. The main reason they aren't usually seen is that scuds have nocturnal habits which tend to make them seek the shadows during the day. Sometimes, when clouds darken the skies, or, late in the evening, they scud along the margins of a lake. Like bunny rabbits, they're prolific but the trout keep them from overcrowding a lake. Gray, brown, tan, olive, and cream are their most common colors. Exact imitations and the Ted Trueblood Otter from numbers 8 to 18 cover most situations. When scuds swim, they are outstretched. Since trout usually feed on the cruising scud, curved hooks aren't necessary. The curling position is the resting position when they aren't highly visible to the trout.

I've disregarded the advice to use long leaders and floating lines and fished my scud patterns on the bottom in depths below 10 feet, and I've paid for it by being fishless. I should resolve to use exact imitations, concentrate in shaded areas near the shoreline, and fish with a weighted pattern on a 10 to 12-foot leader. Slow hand-twists, short smooth pulls, and quick jerks of the line are the best retrieves. I bet it will make a big difference, particularly on my favorite lake where scuds are common. Here's a thought: I've read that although earthworms aren't natural to alpine lakes, if one is dropped into such a lake, a nearby trout dashes for it. Apparently trout smell and recognize favorite foods wherever they swim. Just maybe, since scuds are also favored by trout, a well-presented imitation might be good most anywhere trout live. It's sure worth investigating! Now, I have an excuse to research, even in the cold months, since trout eat scuds in the winter as well as summer.

Facing drop offs and weed beds and casting inward is usually the best strategy, but always be willing to experiment and to learn from those who regularly catch fish. It has worked both ways for me. Many times in Arizona bait or lure fishermen have rowed toward me and asked how I just caught a big trout I released. With blank expressions, it was obvious they didn't believe me when I showed them a number 16 Brown Hackle,

American March Brown, or a number 12 Woolly Worm and explained what the flies represented. Yet, after my move to Sacramento, when I started to learn some of the lakes 90 miles away, I finned toward someone who just released a good-sized cutthroat or rainbow and politely asked how they caught it. A few told me exactly how they did it but others were vague saying it was a "dark-colored" fly and then darted their heads away from me.

Sowbugs, like scuds, are nocturnal. Sometimes anglers call them cressbug or pillbugs. Wide and flat with two long antennae and tails, they are a buggy morsel for a trout to eat. They are usually found in the same habitats where scuds live. Although it is probably the least common type of bug found in trout lakes, a flattened Woolly Worm might be useful now and then. Black and brown in numbers 8 or 10 would do and the retrieve should be slow and even.

These creatures — snails, crayfish, leeches, diving beetles, tadpoles, eels, salamanders, scuds, and sowbugs — which when well-imitated help solve the summer blues. Another group of the "other foods" are not only commonly known but are also obvious to the fishermen when they are on the water. They are the terrestrials. In order to create good dry fly fishing the ants, grasshoppers, and beetles must swarm to the water in masses. My lack of patience keeps me on the bottom and always on the move unless, of course, I find a concentration of surface-feeding trout. But, thus far, in a decade of tubing, I've only run into the flying ant hatch about six times. Grasshoppers create excellent fishing in western streams but, in lakes, they are sporadic, at least where I've fished. Yet it does happen and I have the patterns for such action. When a grasshopper fall occurs, face the shoreline ahead of the cruising trout. Timing and familiarity with a given body of water are the most important factors involved for dry fly terrestrial fishing. It doesn't occur until warm weather (over 80) predominates. Ants normally arrive first in mid to late May. Usually they're black.

The first time I witnessed a flying ant hatch I was amazed. Tubing a lake in Arizona, I glanced at a great big black bug lying in the surface film. Nothing rose to it so I stuck with my sinking line, but finally I stuck my snoot close to the waterline and realized they weren't caddises as I thought. They were flying ants big enough for a number 10 hook! Having just moved from Pennsylvania where ants are tiny, I was amazed. Always hoping for good timing, I carry both flying ants and fur ants in large and small sizes mainly in black.

Twitching a grasshopper imitation as it drifts in the wind is something I try now and then, but the method has yet to work for me mainly because there weren't enough hoppers on the surface to bring up many fish. It is best to observe a trout finning in the shallows and slurping up hoppers struggling in the water. Both the Whitlock and Letort patterns are good in sizes from 10 to 4. Light brown, tan, and olive are the most frequent hopper colors.

The exact same approach is appropriate for fishing with beetles which are usually black or brown and imitated on number 8 or 10 hooks. There are other minor bugs that land in the water throughout the year but they don't usually attract the trout's attention.

Nearly all the bottom and topwater "other foods" discussed in this chapter are found from the West to the East, but they vary with the particular species and degree to which they occur. One must be observant, methodical, and logical when the "other" foods are encountered, but on a quiet summer day when the lake looks depressing, tie on the right imitation and fish it well. I've taken big browns on lakes that were pea-green in color and I thank the summer line-up of bugs and crustaceans for my success.

XIV

Bass Bugging

In most states and bass lakes, largemouth bass average less than four pounds. The relatively few "hawgs" in a given hard-fished lake generally stay in deep water or in thick pods of weeds where heavy bait-casting tackle is at its best. Yet, most books on bass fishing recommend huge popping bugs from numbers 4 to 2/0. If you live in the deep south, Florida, or Texas where bass average four pounds or more but also stay in relatively shallow water, such big popping bugs are worth using, but the rest of us should use more modest-sized bugs. A fisherman who desires to specialize in top water big bassin' should stick to reservoirs with large populations of big bass, learn their haunts, and fish only at night. I think nine out of ten fly fishermen who bass bug enjoy the antics of average-sized bass on light six or seven-weight rods. This chapter is devoted to them.

It took many disappointments throughout the years to realize that bass bugging at dawn wasn't really the best time for catching bass. I did much better late in the afternoon or as the sun set. The main thing for good bass bugging is calm water conditions, shade, and cover like weeds or stumps. Temperature and oxygen content are secondary. At least a million fishing trips too late, I concluded that the "perfect" 70 to 75 degrees seldom held the bass close to the shoreline. My frustration almost drove me crazy as I flung cork or plastic fly rod lures toward the banks of Virginia's Burke Lake, Smith Mountain Lake, and a countless number of small West Virginia and Pennsylvania lakes. If I learned anything (I hope I did!), it was that bass bugging is consistently at its best in farm ponds or in lakes that are less than 20 feet deep and which have weeds, logs, and stumps lining the shorelines. In deeper reservoirs, apparently bass often stay deep even early and late in the day. If they find food in the depths, why should they migrate to the shallows? Bass are just like human beings. Once a largemouth is comfortable on the bottom and has an array of food items near it (or I'm stretched out in the third position of my recliner with a bowl of popcorn on my lap), neither of us are going to move very far.

The first step for bugging a bass is to fish when spring weather first warms the air and the water is close to 65 degrees. On calm days, stay on the shaded sides. If it lacks surface cover, look for underwater weed beds, stumps, rocks, or brush piles and cast toward them. If the bass don't surface, cast next to and parallel with a line of weeds, stumps, or bed of rocks. Take your time. Slow down. Stop kicking. Face the target and fish it well. The idea is to relax, isn't it? Let the bug sit still for as long as humanly possible. If a bass is nearby, chances are it's looking at the thing which just plopped into the water from somewhere in the sky, probably wondering what in the heck it might be. Barely twitch it. If the ripples flatten out inches from the bug, the line strip was perfect, but don't quickly pick up the bug if it wasn't. Let it sit still for a while and jerk lightly on the line again. A pause between short pulls makes the bug resemble an injured moth or minnow. When the artificial reaches deep water, pick up and recast to the other side of the cover or closer to it. If the lake side is barren of cover, tube an easy cast of the shoreline and plop the cork-bodied "fly" next to it. Barely finning along, retrieve and cast with the bank. The idea is to keep the bug near the edges of things whether it be stick ups or the side of the lake. If the slow retrieve fails to bring a response, make the bug pop in the water but be careful. It's too easy to scare wary bass into the depths with too much noise.

When changing from one bug to another, I think it's better to select a different type rather than another color. The most familiar type is the one with a hollow dished-out face which allows it to nose into the water when it is pulled and makes a plopping noise. Bullethead bugs are flat at the front and have a hackle and feathers at the back. It is a "swimmer" which snakes nicely through weeds. Deer hair bugs land with a quiet splat and are good when the bass are highly skittish. Hair-bug types can be gurgled, swum, skittered, or even drifted on wavelets wrinkling the surface. A serious bass bugger should carry all three types in sizes from 4 to 10. I tend to use number 8 the most since they not only cast well but also land quietly on the water. For good hooking, any bug should be tied on a 3XL hook. I've taken bass to three pounds on them as well as large bluegill.

.Muddler Minnows can be used on top much like a Rapala. One excellent technique with them is to cast to a likely place for a bass, let it sit still, pull it under the surface, and pause to let it rise to the surface. I've never skittered a muddler but I bet it works. Experiment and come up with your own retrieves.

Black, yellow, red and white, red and yellow, and blue and white are among the most popular colors. Remember, though, bass only see the bottom shade! Picking a color that is highly visible for the fisherman ought to be the main thing. A dark bottom gives the bass a clear silhouette of the lure.

The least likely fly to present to a bass is a dry fly, but a bushy Irresistable, Wulff, or Bivisible are worth trying. They can be drifted in small waves, gurgled like a hair bug, twitched, inched along, cast toward a rising fish, or skittered on the surface. Numbers 6 to 10 catch not only bass but also panfish.

As I grew up in my teens, I loved to anchor the boat and cast shoreward with cork-bodied fly rod lures as I tried to coax bass to hit them. I still remember the spray of water when a bass burst into the air. Visions of bass thrashing their heads in the air are emblazoned in my mind. Fishing with my dad, Ken Townsend, Bill Crofford, and other good friends are a large part of my bass bugging memories. But, I now know that such fishing is a "minor" tactic which is at its best for brief periods of a season or day. For all day fishing, I stick with the Wet Cel II. On a bass lake, though, my second rod is up with...a bass bug!

XV

Tubing In Wet Weather

The best thing about fishing in the rain is being alone but I don't understand why fishermen leave a lake simply because of inclement weather. It's sensible to quit when the storm is full of electrical energy but a steady rainfall presents no real threat to an angler who is prepared for it. Once I'm on a lake and settled in my tube, I'm there to stay until darkness overtakes the earth. As a thunderstorm develops, I quickly note how far away it is and how fast it is approaching. I keep fishing until the lightning zig-zags over the hills and into the valley where I'm located. At that time, I head for the shoreline but continue to fish as I watch the approaching storm. The shoulder straps go on so when the storm is too close I can step out of the lake quickly. Much too often I'm nowhere near my car.

One time, on Arizona's Sunrise Lake, a storm whipped into a sudden frenzy and, before my next breath, streaks of yellow energy cracked open the dark sky and the thunder boomed with enough force to scare the trout out of the lake. In the next instant as I throttled my legs into high gear toward the shoreline, a trout hit my Zug Bug and another flash of energy streaked right above me. I played a good-sized rainbow in record time, released it, and nearly jumped out of the lake. Breathing heavily, I dropped the tube off my shoulders and plopped my backside onto the hard ground. As I scanned the high-desert plateau surrounding me, I realized that my head was the highest point around the lake. Lying down, I was glad for the neoprene waders and the green rain jacket. The cool air nipped at my nose and cheeks but I was dry. The brick-hard ground prevented mud from forming. The feel of it was cold but the heck if I was going to sit up. I remember thinking that I wasn't frightened. Nature and her creatures aren't to be feared but to be respected.

I laid still looking up at the fireworks crackling and resonating deep sounds across the sky as I smiled thinking not only of the intensity of a storm at almost 9,000 feet but also how nutty I could be.

I honestly don't recommend anyone to be a daredevil like me but I do suggest that a fly rodder should stay on the water throughout most non-electrical storms. If nothing else, on a hot summer day, the cooler air feels good. I've tried to correlate trout activity and behavior with storms of various intensities. I have found some general truths that are applicable most anywhere I've fished from the West to East coast.

Cold steady spring rains keep many fish species on the bottom probably because the lake water is already cold and the rain lowers the temperature a bit more. The light warm rains of early summer are pleasant and the fish continue their usual activities. If bass are in the shallows, they migrate to the depths but trout move only to the edge. All fish are excited when a thunderstorm approaches and they often go crazy hammering my fly on almost every cast until the rain actually drops. The action then slows down but they still hit the fly. Sometimes rain is in scattered drops. At that time, fish remain active but when the rain bursts down and remains steady, they stop hitting. I keep fishing though. I didn't drive 80 or 200 miles to sit in my car and twiddle my fingers. If I hadn't already worn a jacket or rain slicker, before the rain crashes down, I get it out of the back pocket and slip it on. When the weather is cold, I combine the rain slicker with a jacket. Combined with the neoprene waders high up on my chest, I'm almost cozy. I always wear a blue denim cowboy hat when I tube since it protects me from the glare of the sun and the rain. Perhaps it looks silly but, in heavy storms, after cinching the drawstrings of the hood on the rain jacket, I put the cowboy hat back on my head. There is no other place for it and it provides a bigger visor for keeping the rain off my glasses and neck. In the coldest rains of early spring and late fall, I wear a rainproof, heavy nylon coat with a hood.

Sometimes early and late in the year, hail drops on me and covers my stripping apron! I shake my head wondering about my sanity and continue fishing. Intermittently, I use gloves until I'm forced to keep them on. With the short finger holes, my upper fingers are exposed but it still is difficult to retrieve well. By tucking them in a small corner of a gear pocket until warm weather arrives, they're always handy. Now in California, I have an alternative − fish in foothill or valley lakes where the air is warmer. To keep eastern, mid-western, and Rocky Mountain fishermen from envying me, I won't tell of Northern California's warm dry spring and fall weather, but that's why I'm here! It's my way of making up for many years in Missouri, Virginia, Pennsylvania, and Arizona.

Most fishermen seem to prefer catching bass or trout but, since they tend to be sluggish in heavy rains, if catfish and other bottom-hugging species are in the lake, tie on the biggest and ugliest nymph or bucktail and fish it dead slow on the bottom. Channel catfish hit flies, fight well, and taste good. Sometimes I catch one when I least expect it. I might as well enjoy the fight of any kind of fish if I'm slugging out a rain storm!

Now, what everybody must be wondering…what is the best fly and method for fishing in the rain? No one pattern or type has proved itself to be the most effective. Dry flies are definitely out. Now and then, at the beginning of a storm when big raindrops plop into the water every few minutes, trout might surface but bass seem to disappear the moment rain falls. Yet, bass hit better after a rain than trout.

Method is more important than pattern during rainstorms. In a hard rain, I stick to the deepest and clearest parts of a lake. If it has a rock dam or rocky areas, I head for it since the water in such places is likely to remain much clearer than shallow mud banks or weedy regions. The very best place is deep water near food shelves with gravel-lined bottoms.

One theory is that big flies can be seen better in rain storms but, since I've caught both smallmouth and trout on number 12 flies during rainfall, I think it's more important to fish a section of a lake thoroughly; and worry less about patterns. In a hard rain, the fly must be presented as close to a fish as possible. It's also a good idea to keep track of weather patterns and head for a lake known well if rain is predicted. On such a lake, head for the places where the fish rest. When exploring, tube deepwater regions off different points, ledges, and embankments until the fish are found. With long searching casts and slow retrieves, bump the fly on the rocks and brush and snake it through weedbeds.

Marabou bucktails compete with Hare's Ear and Gray nymphs but, keep in mind, no one type or pattern really is consistently effective when rains falls. Regardless of the weather, form a system for choosing fly patterns and for keeping track of what flies were used. I have a separate box for flies I snipped off the leader. Later, when I write in my log book, I don't have to rely on my memory. It takes thought and discipline (especially in rain), but it's worth doing. My log book, started in 1970, has been the source for most of this book and other writings.

I've even tubed when snow flurried in the wind. The water at Rainbow Lake was about 48 and the air was colder, but I had just driven 3½ hours to get there. As I rigged up, my breath frosted in the air and I laughed at myself.

Later, finning down the center of the lake, I looked skyward wondering what was twirling about in the wind. A moment later, a trout hit my number 12 Zug Bug and I soon released a foot-long brown. An hour later I quit not wanting to be stuck on snowy roads.

Dressed well, I wasn't cold except for maybe my hands and face. I don't really like such weather and I avoid fishing in snow storms mainly for not wanting to drive in it, but I proved to myself that trout need to feed regardless of the weather and, that where it is legal, it is worth fishing trout lakes which don't freeze in the winter. Such fishing is slow and deep. Mid-lake regions near feeding areas are the best bet and peacock-bodied flies from the Zug Bug to wet brown hackles and brown or black peacock Woolly Worms are good patterns to use in sizes from 12 to 16. Just why, I don't know. Maybe the irridescent-green flashing in the water attracts the trout's attention. The best retrieve is dead slow. When the cadence of the retrieve is slow enough to send me to dreamland, I know I'm fishing properly. Fishing in the middle with casts parallel to the shoreline do well in rain and snow.

The worst thing about rain is that sometimes, despite how well I dress, it makes me wet and cold but I know I have a change of clothes in my station wagon. Sometimes, a cold develops but, what the heck, I always muck my way through it. Fishing in wet weather brings a satisfaction and contentment which gives me a strong sense of self-reliance even when I fail to catch a fish. Knowing I successfully battled the elements is a good feeling. When I catch good fish, I almost feel smug.

XVI

The "Perfect" Fly

It can be tied in shades from gaudy to somber, with thick to thin bodies, and on long or short-shanked hooks. The fly works for any fish species and can be used in any situation imaginable by fishermen. It is, for these reasons, my favorite fly for exploring new lakes or streams because it can imitate a large variety of insects, bugs, crustaceans, and fish life. This pattern is also one of the oldest in the history of fly fishing and yet is still commonly used by modern fly rodders. I am reasonably certain Thomas Barker in 1657 wrote of it in his *Barker's Delight of The Art of Angling:*

"There are several kinds of Palmers... First, a black Palmer, ribbed with silver. Secondly, a black Palmer ribbed with an orenge-tawny body. Thirdly, a black Palmer made of all black. Fourthly, a red Palmer ribbed with gold. Fifthly, a red Palmer mixed with an orenge-tawny body of cruell. All these flyes must be made with

hackles, and they will serve all the year long morning and evening, windy or cloudy. Without these flyes you cannot make a dayes angling good."

I wish I had the complete text. This quote comes from a segment of this Old-English book, I received from my godfather many years ago. At an early age, I was strongly impressed with the long tradition of my favorite sport. Today we call the fly the Woolly Worm.

Whenever I'm on a lake and too many fishless hours skip by (even on slow days my fishing time goes too fast), and my confidence level is near zero, my spirits are boosted high when I tie on a Woolly Worm. Thinking back on such days, I now realize my lack of success was due to four things – not having picked the best lake possible to fish, wasting time on areas of the lake without fish, not employing the best fishing strategy, or from a bad choice of a fly pattern.

On a recent trip to a favorite Sierra Nevada mountain lake my frustrations were keen after six fishless hours. Other boaters and tubers were catching big rainbows and browns. Each one of them had a very different opinion of what to do and what fly was best. One boater swore it was a day for large bucktails stripped quickly toward the shore and on the bottom. One tuber caught his fish imitating a midge hatch which – was only breaking up the small fish. The man in the boat said he brought in browns to five pounds. I can be cynical at times, but I believed he caught and released them at this fish-for-fun lake. Having seen such trout caught here helped me have trust in his words. A fellow walking the bank told me he fished here only at day break and that he never stayed on the water much after 9:00 a.m. which was about when I began my day. Somebody else told me not to worry about the hatches and to concentrate on the bottom with nondescript patterns. There was a day when all this would have confused me, but now I accept it as the wonderful complexities of trout fishing which I love more with each new trip I make. However, that was one of those days when it probably would have been easier on my temperament to have gone home and finally cleaned my apartment, did the laundry, or went job hunting!

On that day on my favorite trout lake, I stuck with nymphs when I observed various hatches. Since the lake held trout to six pounds, I didn't concern myself with adult forms. I had decided the big ones stayed down to feed on the immature forms of these insects. But my underwater strategies weren't working. I tried several bucktails but that didn't do it either. Finally I opened the black Wheatly box devoted to Woolly Worms. I scanned over many shades tied mostly on number 8 and number 12, 3XL hooks. In fact, I recently concluded that I needed to add larger sizes to my collection since I live in the central valley of California where I am literally surrounded by bass reservoirs, many of which are also stocked with trout in the winter. In the biggest lakes, the rainbows grow large and survive the hot summer by escaping into the depths. But, most of the time, when I trout fish the mountain lakes which are usually clear, the smaller flies work best.

Since I already used dark and dull nymph patterns, I only gazed over the black and brown Woolly Worms. Noticing the dark green ones, I contemplated using one, but then I thought most of my success with a green Woolly Worm was early in the year before the damsel fly naiads rose toward the surface. The gray body, brown hackle Woolly caught my attention and I remembered they often worked when my brown ones failed. I almost put one on, but something stopped me. I wasn't sure what. We anglers, as scientific as we become, should never forget our intuitions, our hunches. It was such a feeling that helped me catch my biggest Arizona White Mountain trout, a fat 19-inch brown. The smallest "palmer" in gray worked well when a caddis or midge hatched. The Woolly with bright yellow chenille and brown hackle tempted me. A moment later I pulled one of them out of the box and I knotted the number 12 fly to the tippet. With my first cast, my depression quickly lifted and my energies were renewed. I cast it all around me as I sat in the float tube and faced the shoreline opposite the car. I finned toward the weedy side, but a few minutes later, a fish hit the fly. After a short but violent fight, I brought in a foot-long rainbow. I admired its shine and iridescent lateral gleam thinking that hatchery trout never glisten quite like that. One of the men on shore watched me. I smiled and enjoyed being observed. Happiness filled me with this pleasant reversal. Soon another trout struck. Is the Woolly Worm magic, or what?

I honestly don't know why a trout would hit such a Woolly Worm. Maybe the bright shade attracts its attention and the fish is curious what it might be. In order to find out it must engulf the object since fish don't have hands like we humans do. They quickly spit out anything inedible. I have heard and read that some fishermen think such a Woolly Worm imitates wasps or bumblebees but these insects float. Nearly always, I crawl my flies on the bottom. I know there are some yellow caddis fly larvae and maybe that's what the trout have in mind when they take the yellow Woolly, but I've yet to do a stomach autopsy to confirm my theory. I won't stick my neck out concerning this matter until I've done more research.

Next I tried a peacock herl-brown Woolly Worm. From conversations with people, this appears to be a combination not used much. It ought to be! Frequently it works wonders on choosy trout. My guess is the fragility of this body material makes the fly unpopular. Personally, I'll take any pattern for its ability to catch trout over its durability. The bright green body and brown hackle, I think, is reminiscent of many bugs that crawl on lake bottoms or dive up and down in the water. Despite the similarities to the Zug Bug, I know there have been days when one fly works better than the other. When neither caught fish, the smaller brown hackle wet fly tied with peacock herl produced the action.

But, today, it didn't show off its charm and, as the sun lowered to the edge of the earth, I tied on an all-black pattern. Consistently, the dark color brings me good results at this time of day. We fly fishermen know when to change patterns that imitate flies that are easily observable in the air or are close to the surface, but down deep in lakes, we are unable to know exactly what is going on. In fact, I think that is what attracts me to lake fly fishing.

As I probed the main channel of the lake, I thought that perhaps various bugs, crustaceans, and nymphs came out from hideouts at different hours of the day and that maybe something dark and ugly like leeches started moving about late in the day and therefore the dark-colored flies worked best as the sun lowered toward the horizon. Mind you, it's only a theory. Perhaps I should get scuba gear and verify!

A trout slurped up my fly. But when I struck, the fish surged away and pulled free from the hook. I don't dare repeat what I said! It had great power and I thought it might have been a huge brown. At least, that was what I wanted to believe.

Yet I still had my fly on the 4X tippet. Often such a light taper is hazardous for playing big fish, but I usually get more strikes because of it.

It was my last strike of the day. Darkness descended as I stowed my gear and headed for home. Since it was the Woolly Worm which brought me luck, I reflected, as I drove, on some conclusions I came to on fishing Woolly Worms in lakes in Arizona and California over the past 10 years.

Nearly all the Woolly Worms which I have seen in sporting goods stores are thick, heavily-hackled creatures. On the whole, they are ineffective for most trout fishing. Nine times out of ten, a thin dressing with only a whisper of a hackle catches not only the most but also the biggest trout. I find this is particularly true in clear, hard-fished lakes, With visibilities of more than four feet. Lowering something bright on a long cord marked with a knot at intervals of a foot is an easy way to determine this fishing variable. When I compare fish totals with anglers throughout the summer months, nearly always, I have done much better than them, simply and only because I use small flies and slow retrieves.

I have received many stares from them when I said I caught my fish on a brown Woolly Worm.

"But that's what I used!" many of them remarked.

Not really. Often I saw their Woolly Worm on their leader. Those mammoth flies looked like the meanest caterpillar this side of the Mississippi River! Such dressings do have their place in muddy water, late in the fall, and for bass, steelhead or salmon, and other big fish. But for consistent results for trout up to 20 inches, I use numbers 8 and 12 with the emphasis on the latter. They are tied with the thinnest chenille possible and with only a fluff of a hackle.

With the proper two-tone colors for the body and chenille and tied a bit bulkier, a Woolly Worm becomes a stonefly imitation. I recall one time fishing a lake in Arizona when the men trolling such flies did better than me. It always pays to experiment. Thinking of that day with hindsight, I now realize that I was in a rut with my small fly adage. This is another reason for me to expand my sizes, dressings, and shades this year, yet I know that at least 75 percent of the time, the small flies in all-brown, all-black, dark green with brown hackle, and gray with brown hackle are the most effective.

But, of course, the Woolly Worm is not invariably the best fly to use. I still have many other flies for close "match the hatch" work and other strategies. Yet, the next time I fish, I will probably begin and end my day with the Woolly Worm!

The "Real" Reason
For Float Tubing

It would be great to be rich and have all the tackle you ever wanted, wouldn't it? Although I have accumulated a wide assortment of gear in the past 20 years, somewhere along the way, I realized fish could be caught without owning a tackle shop worth of gear. Before fishing from a float tube, I waded the lakes of Arizona's White Mountains. Because of easy access and a gravel bottom, I concentrated on Becker Lake. The spell of its rainbow trout, streaking far toward the middle, haunted me even when I performed my humdrum duties as a bookstore clerk.

One of my best days was in June when the sun cooked the thin mountain air as a wind whipped a froth of waves across the lake's surface. Refusing to let such weather bother me, I rigged up my seven-weight 8½-foot rod, slipped my waders and vest on, and hiked the trail which took me to my favorite spot. As I walked along, I listened to ducks and birds create a symphony of song. Noticing two boaters, I wondered how they were doing. The electric motors quietly putted them along the shoreline opposite me. Summertime is a good season to be alone on a trophy-fishing lake, but in April, there are enough boats on it to let me walk from one side to the other.

Now in June, the main problem of wading Becker Lake was the thick mat of weeds which lined the banks throughout most of the warm months, but today, the weed-beds weren't quite at their peak. When I reached my "fishing hole," I slogged through a thick carpet of weeds and moss. Halfway through the watery jungle, I suddenly stepped into water halfway up my fly vest.

"Whoa!"

I glanced around glad to know nobody heard my shout. With only my upper chest, neck, and head out of the water, I must have been a strange sight but I was determined to catch trout come hell...or weeds! As I backed up, I thought I detected trout rising in the open water. With the waves, I couldn't be sure. June was a good month for caddises and damselflies.

With a glance to my right, I glimpsed at a mountain ridge with a dusting of snow on the peaks. The smoky-gray ridge etched itself across the landscape and the bright blue sky.

Wearing a lightweight jacket for sudden rainstorms, I didn't worry about my elbows poking into the water as I pulled the wet Dark Cahill from the keeper guide and readied myself to cast. In short sharp strokes, I worked out line. When the fly and line dropped, I zipped the fly back toward me until it reached the edge of the weed-bed not quite 15 feet from where I stood. As I false cast, I hoped to find a rising trout but I didn't. Fancasting from left to right, I worked the water around me. On my tenth retrieve, a fish socked the fly and it dashed for the middle but, soon enough, I released a heavily-muscled 16-inch rainbow trout. A small opening in the weeds helped me bring the fish my way.

Bending over a bit, I scrutinized the surface trying to confirm my belief. Yes, I could barely notice an insect buzzing just above the waterline. It was the brown caddis hatch I expected.

For me, that is sufficient. There are enough Schwiebert's and LaFontaine's in the world. I don't need to be one. I enjoy reading their books and try to understand every aspect of my sport as possible. The swept-back style of the winged wet fly was close in form to the caddis bursting out of the water. The fast erractic strip approximated the behavior of the live insect well enough to fool the trout, at least for today!

Another trout hit but it shook the fly as it leaped into the air and laughed at me. I recast and slopped a bit of water with my elbow but 15 feet away it wasn't noticeable. I fired out a cast toward another riser. The trout struck on my first line pull and I reacted quicker. The trout sky-rocketed into the air several times and played tug-of-war with me for a while before I slipped the hook out of its mouth and watched it swim toward the depths.

A muscle cramp in my lower left leg bothered me but I didn't dare move since I could easily create a mudline which could drift toward the trout. I ignored it and continued with my fishing. Before the hatch ended, I landed six rainbows from 14 to 17 inches.

When I turned toward the bank about 20 feet away, my left leg momentarily stiffened and I slipped toward the deep water. The thick mat of weeds actually held me upright! Since I've been a good swimmer all my life, I've never feared deep water. Nevertheless, I was startled for a moment. With a strap cinched high around my waders, water would stay out and I'd probably float.

Quickly I regained confidence and I slowly stepped backwards. Holding onto the strong cords which anchored the weeds to the bottom, I kept myself from tripping. Fifteen minutes later, I was on the bank and I walked to another stretch of shoreline where there were less weeds.

I stopped wading just as the water crept above my waistline. My elbows stayed clear of the water and casting was easier. Here, the bottom contoured toward the depths quickly and I wished I had a sinking line. Now I have several.

With a 10-foot leader and weighted flies, I managed to reach the bottom and caught several more rainbows well over a foot. In fact, this is the method Brian Clarke prefers. In *The Pursuit of Stillwater Trout*, he details how he fishes deep water by using leaders in excess of 20 feet. I think that is clumsy, but heck, if we all fished the same way, we couldn't argue with each other! I used his system with leaders to 12 feet until I could afford extra spools and sinking lines.

When darkness descended, I had landed 10 trout, one of which went to 18 inches.

I love tubing and being able to reach 30-foot depths but I won't let myself forget those days before I owned this nice gear. If I'm caught short without a tube or fins, I know how to continue in my mad pursuit for trout and bass. At my most intrepid level of courage, I once stepped into 50-degree water wearing only jeans. I caught some of the trout rising on the other side of the weeds but I also went home sneezing and coughing.

But I'm not totally crazy. When I stare at a cliff jutting straight down to deep water only two feet from the side of the lake, I won't attempt to wade. And that's the "real" reason for float tubing!

The Flies For Lake Fishing

Fly tying — I tried it and didn't like it! After several attempts to persuade myself that all serious fly fishermen "rolled" their own, I concluded that, when not fishing I'd rather write, read, play my tenor saxophone, and do other various things. I know the advantage of fly tying and I've witnessed a few fly rodders who tied the imitation of the evening hatch on their tailgates and I admire them but most of the time the standard patterns work fine. Here is a listing of patterns which are easily found in most fly shops or catalogs. I highly doubt if I am the only non-tying member of sub-species *Sapien fly fisher* who is tired of looking at meticulous dressings for a million variations of the same fly.

NYMPHS

They should be tied sparsely, slim, and unweighted. Using lead underneath the bodies not only makes them too bulky and hard to cast but also makes them behave unnaturally in the water. I recommend numbers 12 to 20.

Hare's Ear (also available in olive and black); Gray; Zug Bug; Beaver; American March Brown (my snail imitation); Midge Pupa (black, gray, and yellow); Midge Larvae; Light Cahill; Dark Cahill; Mosquito Larva; Mosquito Pupa; Scud (tan, gray, cream); Pheasant Tail; Trueblood's Otter; *Callibaetis*; Breadcrust; Tellico; All purpose nymphs (dark, medium, and light); Caddis Pupa; Caddis Larva; Grouse Wing Backswimmer; Micro-Caddis; Jannsen Damsel; Whitlock Crayfish.

Of all these flies, I recommend a beginner to start with the Hare's Ear, Gray, Zug Bug, Beaver, tan Scud, and black Midge Pupa. Size 12 and 16 are best except for the midge which should be number 20. It's smart to check with local experts. In the Sierra Nevada range east of Sacramento, yellow and red midge pupa are important. The simplest style is the best.

WOOLLY WORMS

They should be lightly hackled and with thin bodies on number 8 and 12 for trout. For bass, thicker dressings on number 4 and 6 are good.

All-black; All-brown; All-purple; Brown with peacock herl; Black with peacock herl; Gray and grizzle hackle; Yellow with brown hackle; Tan with brown hackle; Green with brown hackle; Olive with brown hackle; White with brown hackle; Orange with brown hackle; Purple with black hackle; Black with grizzle hackle.

A basic collection is all-brown; all-black; brown with peacock herl; gray with grizzle hackle; yellow with brown hackle; and green with brown hackle.

BUCKTAILS AND STREAMERS

I like numbers 8 and 12 for trout and numbers 4 and 6 for bass. Number 8 is the best all-round size for any kind of fishing.

All-black Marabou; All-brown Marabou; Brown and white Marabou; All-black Woolly Bugger; All-brown Woolly Bugger; All-green Woolly Bugger; Black over gray Woolly Bugger; Yellow over brown Woolly Bugger; Black over purple Woolly Bugger; Brown over orange Woolly Bugger; Dark Spruce

Streamer; Light Spruce Streamer; Brown Matuka; Black Matuka; Muddler Minnow.

I found hair-wing bucktails like the Mickey Finn and Black Nosed Dace are ineffective when lake fishing yet I have some with me. One never knows! A basic four is the Muddler Minnow; Black Marabou; Dark Spruce; and brown Woolly Bugger.

WET FLIES

Sizes 12 to 16 are the best. They are in three groups — hackle, feather, and winged.

Adams; Light Cahill; Dark Cahill; Quill Gordon.

Black Gnat (black wing is better); Coachman; Leadwing Coachman; Hare's Ear (not gold ribbed); Pale Evening Dun; Montreal; Fur Ants; McGinty; Western Bee.

Brown Hackle (peacock); Brown hackle, yellow body; Brown hackle, brown silk body; Gray hackle, yellow body (segmented with windings of thread); Gray hackle, gray body.

Always carry brown hackle, peacock; Gray hackle-yellow; Adams; Dark Cahill; Leadwing Coachman; and Hare's Ear.

DRY FLIES

Sizes 12 to 20 are the best. For bass try numbers 6 to 10.

Adams; Flying Ant (black); Wingless Ants; Henry's Fork Hopper; Letort Hopper; Whitlock Hopper; Light Cahill; Dark Cahill; Black (hackle) Midge; Brown (hackle) Midge; Gray (hackle) Midge; Brown Bivisible; Black Bivisible.

Sticking only with the Adams, ants, Black Midge, and a hopper pattern covers a lot of territory.

POPPING BUGS

Gaines and Whitlock are two of the best manufacturers. Include deer body and hard-bodied ones. Have concave bugs, and flat-faced ones on 3XL hooks from 4 to 10.

All-Black; All-yellow; Red and white; and Blue and white are the most recommended.

Exact brand names as long as they are reputable, to me, are secondary.

I didn't mean to miss your favorite patterns. Remember, this isn't an encyclopedia of flies. For a non-tier, I have strange ideas of how flies should be tied, don't I? I like what works! I just realized it takes a tier (or tier friend) to have the variations I list.

The Skillful Tuber

But, in the main, these flies are readily available. With these basic flies, a "skillful" tuber who learned all the strategies in this book is going to catch big trout, bass, and panfish.

It's been great tubing with you. Let's do it again, okay?